OSKAR KOKOSCHKA

Herodotos

OSKAR KOKOSCHKA

Edited by

Klaus Albrecht Schröder and Johann Winkler

With essays by

Christoph Asendorf, Ingried Brugger, Edwin Lachnit
and Johann Winkler

Prestel

First published in German on the occasion of the exhibition
'Oskar Kokoschka' at the Kunstforum Länderbank, Vienna,
14 March to 23 June 1991

Translated from the German by David Britt

Cover:
The Power of Music, 1920 (plate 42)

Frontispiece:
Self-Portrait as Herodotus, 1961;
drawing for the front page of the *Times Literary Supplement*

Photograph on page 9:
Kokoschka in his studio at Villeneuve
on Lake Geneva, 1960; on the easel is a painting of Herodotus
(Photo: Gertrude Fehr, Territet)

© Prestel-Verlag, Munich, 1991
© of illustrated works by Oskar Kokoschka:
VG Bild-Kunst, Bonn, and COSMOPRESS, Geneva, 1991;
Otto Dix: Dix Erben, Baden, Switzerland;
George Grosz and Vasily Kandinsky:
VG Bild-Kunst, Bonn
Photographic Acknowledgments: page 230

Prestel-Verlag, Mandlstrasse 26, D-8000 Munich 40,
Germany

Distributed in continental Europe by Prestel-Verlag,
Verlegerdienst München GmbH & Co KG,
Gutenbergstrasse 1, D-8031 Gilching, Germany

Distributed in the USA and Canada by te Neues Publishing Company,
15 East 76th Street, New York, NY 10021, USA

Distributed in Japan by YOHAN-Western Publications Distribution Agency,
14-9 Okubo 3-chome, Shinjuku-ku, J-Tokyo 169

Distributed in the United Kingdom, Ireland and all other countries by
Thames & Hudson Limited, 30-34 Bloomsbury Street, London WC1 B3QP, England

Composition by Max Vornehm, Munich
Offset lithography by Reproduktionsgesellschaft Karl Dörfel mbH, Munich
Printed and bound by Passavia Druckerei GmbH, Passau

Printed in Germany
ISBN 3-7913-1132-8 (English edition)
ISBN 3-7913-1123-9 (German edition)

Contents

Foreword

Oskar Kokoschka's historical significance has long been generally recognized, but, curiously, few specialist studies have appeared to give proper weight to that recognition. There is no standard work on the birth of modernism that fails to lay due emphasis on Kokoschka's contribution, no survey of Expressionism in which he is not given ample space. Last but not least, none of the art historical *tours d'horizon* on the phenomenon of 'Vienna 1900' fails to discover in Kokoschka's early work traces of what has been dubbed *Experiment Weltuntergang*, the End of the World Experiment.

Yet a trawl through the libraries and bibliographies for monographs on Kokoschka will yield very little of real value apart from, say, Edith Hoffmann's biography and Hans Maria Wingler's *catalogue raisonné* of the paintings. The last strictly art historical study to be published was the monograph by Fritz Schmalenbach, which was restricted to formal analysis. And these three works all date from the 1940s and 1950s. The many subsequent collections of anecdotes, based on more or less significant encounters with the artist, would be most appropriately assigned to the literary genre of hagiography.

Paradoxical or not, some of the responsibility for this distortion of Kokoschka's reputation in his own lifetime must be laid at his own door. When that meticulous chronicler, Edith Hoffmann, showed him the first, ultimately unpublished draft of her book, he told her that she had sacrificed his 'uniqueness' to a petty-minded concern with artistic influences:

> If it had been the way you describe it, I would at the very least have had to hang around museums and libraries and academies all my life, instead of doing what every original artist pursues with utter single-mindedness: to let himself live in the present, opening his eyes wherever he—and not the art reporter—is constrained to look and listen. I can't describe to you what I have seen, but in any case it is not what you try to convince yourself and others in this book that it is. All very well for the likes of your precious Schiele, of course, but in my case well below my cost price.

It is possible to have some sympathy with Kokoschka's idiosyncratic aversion to the art historian's pursuit of derivations, which he dismissed as an anti-artistic attempt to tame and familiarize the strange and the outlandish. Yet it is only by seeing and interpreting art in its context that we can ever bring out what is specific in it. Just how unwise it is to take the artist's self-portrayal, and the level of contemporary response, at face value clearly emerges from Christoph Asendorf's essay in this book, which traces the early critics' recurrent metaphors for Kokoschka's visionary power back to their factual basis: the shock of realizing, through the discoveries of science, that matter itself is permeable.

A contextual interpretation of Kokoschka also corrects the widely held idea that he was an 'apolitical' artist. This supposition, extrapolated from his own caustic criticisms of revolutionary goings-on in Dresden, has caused his subsequent political allegories of the Second World War to be regarded as a totally isolated phenomenon. Only a careful iconological interpretation of this group of works, and its integration into the overall pattern of Kokoschka's allegorical thinking, can uncover the distinctive evolutionary continuity of his work.

This brings us to the true reason for the art historians' neglect of Kokoschka's work as a whole: it presents the distressing spectacle of a creative process that appears to be discontinuous, of an *oeuvre* that lacks homogeneity. The same goes for the career of Giorgio de Chirico, with its drastic changes of direction, and for the late work of Picasso, which was long dismissed as senile banality. In artists who die young, such as Egon Schiele, August Macke or Umberto Boccioni, life and work are rounded off and neatly correlated; but in long-lived artists the anachronism of synchronicity, the generation gap that brings individual evolution out of step with general evolution, and the natural divergences between early and late work, tend to impose an unconscionable strain. This pattern, which bears no relation to the degree of success enjoyed by the artist in his own lifetime, can be traced in the careers of such disparate artists as Georges Braque, Marc Chagall and Max Beckmann.

In Kokoschka's case the artist's fidelity to figurative painting—and his uncompromising rejection of all that was *informel* or otherwise abstract—only served to confirm the apparently obvious. There emerged a universal consensus that his early Expressionism had occupied a necessary historical niche, but that, since the late 1920s, if not before, by remaining doggedly faithful to it he had fallen out of step with his times.

It was not until the 1980s, when the craving for images returned, the easel painting was rehabilitated and artists once more felt free to paint gesturally, that attention fastened on Kokoschka's work after the mid-1950s. Above all, the founder members of the German *Neue Wilden* (the 'New Fauves') discovered in Kokoschka's late painting the vestiges of an artistic ethos that was of vital importance to them. Thus, Georg Baselitz, for example, lent his support to Kokoschka's late painting against over-hasty attempts to dismiss it in favour of *Art informel*, Op Art or Conceptual Art. Baselitz directly traced his own conception of art back to Kokoschka and thereby pointed to the unbroken continuity of a figurative, gestural, expressive tradition in art. This recent declaration of allegiance to Kokoschka's example is far more than a pious gesture; once and for all, it gives the lie to the words that Kokoschka himself, in a moment of profound self-doubt, once noted down in Dresden: 'Everything flourishes; I alone die out'.

Present-day art thus serves to expand our view of this artist's work. The new aspects that emerge are not only correctives to the old, oversimplified conception of Kokoschka's development as an artist; they also alert us to hitherto unobserved connections between the early and late work. The present book, originally published in German on the occasion of a major retrospective exhibition at the Kunstforum in Vienna and expanded to include further plates, reflects this tendency to reassess the affinities between seemingly contradictory formal ideas. The details reproduced in the plates are deliberately chosen to point out analogies of subject and type, with the intention of alerting the viewer to the distinctions as well as the affinities, the identity as well as the uniqueness, in the painting of Oskar Kokoschka.

Klaus Albrecht Schröder

Christoph Asendorf

'Lurching Space'

The Early Work, 1907-1916

I

In 1898 Adolf Loos published his essay 'Das Prinzip der Bekleidung' (The Principle of Clothing). In it he took Gottfried Semper's assertion that the art of weaving was the first and original art and used it to argue that anyone who wants a space to live in must first visualize the carpets, design the floors and walls, and only then devise the structural framework.[1] Architecture, for Loos, was a garment, made to clothe not a solid body but a space. That space was thus designed from the inside outwards; it was created by a process of wrapping, not of hollowing out. Thinking from the inside outwards, starting with the space and not with the carcass of the building: this was a radical reversal of the architect's viewpoint.

In 1933, in his funeral oration for Loos, Kokoschka reminded his hearers of this frontal assault on the skin-deep aesthetic of the *fin de siècle*, this determination to build houses 'outwards from within . . . with a spatial plan instead of a fine facade'.[2] A spatial idea that had been rigorously thought through, with ceiling heights varied according to use and economically arranged communication areas, so that the house becomes an organism conceived from the inside, could dispense with an ornate facade. It was precisely this that caused the controversy which greeted Loos's building on Michaelerplatz in Vienna. The customary criteria of architectural quality had simply been ignored, and the profoundly innovative qualities of the structure were concealed within. In such a building architecture was transformed into topographical anatomy, into the study of positional relationships between individual spatial limbs. Albert Ehrenstein extended this logic of opening up from within to apply to the work of Kokoschka himself, describing him as 'the slicer-open of souls' and his portraits as 'psychotomy'.[3]

Fig. 1, 2 Portraits of Kamilla Swoboda, from *Variations on a Theme*, Vienna, 1921, nos. V, VI; collotypes of drawings from 1920, each 71 x 51 cm

II

Kokoschka's art defines itself negatively: it is the antithesis of Impressionism. A comparison may make this clear. In 1921 Max Dvořák juxtaposed Kokoschka's *Variations on a Theme* (see fig. 1, 2), a series of ten portrait drawings of a young woman listening to music,[4] with Claude Monet's 'Haystack' series (see fig. 3, 4) and deduced a number of criteria that reveal the specific nature of Kokoschka's mode of representation.

Monet's 'Haystacks' were painted between 1888 and 1893; in around thirty variants they depict the haystacks as they pass through successive shifts of light and season. Monet showed fifteen of these paintings at the Galerie Durand-Ruel in 1891, in the first exhibition ever devoted to different representations of a single object. Fully aware that he had reached the limit of what can be done with painting, Monet spoke of his anxiety that, in painting successive effects of light, he would be unable to keep up with the rapidity of change in the environment.

To Dvořák this series represented the triumph of an age that placed its faith in the ability to interpret nature with the implements of science. It was an attitude that found its artistic counterpart in the constant refinement of methods of observing and reproducing nature. By the end of the nineteenth century, however, this naturalistic sensationalism had been shaken to its foundations.

Dvořák's text is an apologia for Expressionism, even though he avoids using that word. He writes in response to the new scientific awareness of the limitations of the senses, in an age of discoveries in electricity and new conceptual models in physics; but the language he uses to articulate the new-found attractions of the supersensible is that of vitalist philosophy. The psyche comes to be seen as the organ of a perception that transcends the sensory. What is to be represented is no longer the evanescent effects of light and atmosphere but 'the stirring of psychic emotion'; and so the human image once more becomes a favoured theme.

That is one aspect of Dvořák's antithesis between Monet's series and Kokoschka's variations. More important, however, is the shift in general approach. To Dvořák Kokosch-

Fig. 4   Claude Monet, *Haystack, Snow Effect, Morning*, 1891; oil on canvas, 65.4 x 92.4 cm. Museum of Fine Arts, Boston

ka's achievement in presenting 'what is transitory and fluctuating in the psyche' is the result of an evolution that began when, 'in an expression of inner, vital experience, sensory perception was utterly, subjectively and arbitrarily transformed'.

Dvořák's reference to a form of vital experience (*Erleben*) transcending sensory perception, which he adopts as a counter to the 'soulless' sensationalism of the nineteenth century, revives a debate that Immanuel Kant had already engaged in, albeit on the opposite side of the fence. Kant's *Träume eines Geistersehers* (Dreams of a Spirit-Seer), published in 1766, was directed particularly against Emanuel Swedenborg and his unbridled use of the speculative faculties. As Kant's critical philosophy took shape, such faculties inevitably fell by the wayside: 'I am conjoined with beings kindred to myself by means of corporeal laws, but whether I am, or ever shall be, conjoined according to other laws which I call spiritual, without the instrumentality of matter, I can in no way conclude from what is given me.'[5]

Expressionism dispensed with this crucial reservation. And Kokoschka added one more to the current stock of terms for supersensible experience. 'Von der Natur der Gesichte' (On the Nature of Visions) is the title of a programmatic lecture that he gave in 1912: 'The awareness of visions is life itself, which chooses among the configurations that come to it, and can hold aloof from what it dislikes.'[6]

To have visions does not mean becoming aware of objects but of oneself in objects. Visions are subject to no constraints of time or space but are entirely at the service of the subjective observer; by denying the exclusive validity of sensory perception, they confirm the validity of supersensible, vital experience.

Reality becomes open to question. Objects drop out of their normal functional contexts. In themselves, the pictorial conception and the arrangement of the objects in Kokoschka's *Still Life with Lamb and Hyacinth* (plate 9) allude to this duality of vision. This is a painting that arose from a rejected invitation to a feast. Kokoschka was to recall[7] how a feeling of revulsion had swept over him at the sight of the skinned

Fig. 3   Claude Monet, *Haystack in Sunlight*, 1891; oil on canvas, 60 x 100 cm. Kunsthaus, Zurich

Easter lamb; it suddenly seemed impossible to eat 'this dead thing'. Instead, he decided to paint it. So he took the cadaver off the kitchen table and into an adjoining lumber room, where he arranged a still life with some accessories from the nursery. An old turtle, an axolotl in an aquarium, a white mouse, a tomato, a battered antique oil-jar and a luminous, white hyacinth set the strangely assorted scene.

The completed painting, with its run-down objects, all diverted from their proper use and all on the point of decay, is an emblem of the dissolution of existing relationships. We are forcibly reminded of Hugo von Hofmannsthal's account of the decay of language in 'The Letter of Lord Chandos' (1901/2). Things that are mentioned in conversation loom in an 'uncanny closeness', writes Hofmannsthal, eluding the 'simplifying eye' of linguistic habit: one sudden pang of disquiet, and this regulatory device of social intercourse stands revealed as unusable. This state of affairs—words and concepts that crumble to nothing in the mouth 'like mouldy fungi' or 'take on iridescent colour, so flowing over into one another'[8]—is the fateful sign of the cultural disintegration described elsewhere, on a panoramic scale, by Alfred Kubin. In Perle, capital of Kubin's imaginary kingdom, mould and decay are rife, and the buildings of the city crumble. Decline and fall are manifest in the 'sickness of inanimate matter'.[9]

For all the obviousness of the affinity, this contextual reference is far from representing the last word on Kokoschka's picture and its aesthetic strategy. The infirmity and instability of the material objects is indeed immediately apparent: the turtle and the oil-jar seem almost to melt into their surroundings; the tomato, although it is positioned in front of the aquarium, seems to surge out of it—its flesh and the water dissolve into each other. The light, without a visible source, is irrationally distributed: the scene is plunged in a diffuse half-light, and yet the lamb, the axolotl and the hyacinth seem to glow from within. The greasy sheen of the lamb's flesh is so powerful that it penetrates the jar. The hyacinth is ringed by a blue, fluorescent aura, like a poisonous miasma. There is almost no indication of space, or even of a firm base, and yet the objects do not hang suspended in a fathomless void: overlapping, they sink into the paint. Their arrangement in a ring, within a pictorial space that seems fluid, suggests a circulatory motion that has been arrested.

III

The image of matter here begins to invite multiple interpretations. Monet had already shown how the optical effect of his 'Haystacks' was constantly modified by the influence of light: the dissolution of apparently stable properties. Like all naturalism, Impressionism is an investigation of the surface of things; the eye of the Symbolist, by contrast, delves into the substance of matter. Finite solids are split open, hollowed out and rendered fluid or permeable. Consistencies are altered. In *My Self-Portrait as a Skeleton* (1889)[10] James Ensor visualizes himself as a death's-head, with a beard and

a haircut, set on a neatly dressed body. The eye pierces through the skin and flesh of the face to the underlying bone structure. In 1906 Alberto Martini illustrated a fantastic tale by Edgar Allan Poe: in *The Conversation of Eiros and Charmion* the human race is wiped out in an explosion of 'dazzling brilliancy' caused by a collision with a comet.[11] Martini's shadowy, reclining figure struggles unavailingly against the 'impalpable gaseous character' of the light that emanates from the heavenly body.

With the discovery of X-rays and radioactivity, a number of basic certainties of perception and of physics had been shaken: the impenetrability of solids, the conservation of energy and the immutability of the elements.[12] These discoveries were soon popularized: as early as 1896 the magazine *Die Gartenlaube* ran a number of articles on X-rays, publishing a photograph in which nothing is visible of the surface of a lady's hand but the shadow of her wedding ring.

In Thomas Mann's novel *The Magic Mountain*, that panoramic view of the years before the First World War, Hans Castorp confronts the problem of the atom, which 'could hardly yet—or hardly still—be thought of as material, but rather as the mean or borderline between the material and the immaterial', as a 'concretion of the insubstantial, of the not-yet-substantial but already substance-like: a concretion of energy'. Mann's 'unassuming' hero is badly shaken by a visit to an X-ray laboratory: 'For two seconds terrible forces were in play, those forces that must be brought to bear in order to penetrate matter'. In the text of the novel this establishment is described as a 'transillumination laboratory', and Mann does not miss the opportunity to make an ironic jab at psychoanalysis, which he describes as a conceptual system (and, by implication, a mechanism, like Röntgen's apparatus) for the 'transillumination of the unconscious'.[13]

Fig. 5 Vasily Kandinsky, *Lady in Moscow*, 1912; oil on canvas, 108.8 x 108.8 cm. Städtische Galerie im Lenbachhaus, Munich

IV

'The Problem of the Portrait' is the title of an essay by Georg Simmel, published in 1918. The age-old question of the validity of outward appearances had returned to the fore at a time when altered ways of seeing had relativized all visual perception. As his starting point Simmel took the general problem of 'visibility'. What we see of a person, his optical appearance, is distinct from what we know—and therefore, in a different sense, see—of him. We complete the picture in the light of our recollections, our immediate concerns, our present state of mind: 'In short, one person is to another a fluctuating complex of sense impressions of all kinds, and of mental associations'.[14]

This goes far beyond the optical. Significantly, the word 'fluctuating' implies a constantly shifting impression; even in purely optical terms, we miss far too much ever to be able to build up a complete picture. Our gaze, both physical and metaphorical, rests on a part of the whole—on a detail, in fact. Simmel extends the problem of visibility on to a sociological level: an essential characteristic of the urban experience is the 'intensification of nervous life', with the consequence that stable relations are supplanted by 'flow and pulsation'.[15]

V

Kokoschka's early work is dominated by portraiture. What strikes us at once is the—metaphorically—naked, exposed look of the sitters. Cut off by the frame, the figures seem lost in an undefined space, with no floor, no fixed background, no tangible setting of any kind to stabilize them. The external conditions of life are neither stylized nor flaunted. Instead, the sitters are shown with an absent look: mostly, their gaze is not directed outwards at all; they are rapt in contemplation of what is going on within.

The rendering visible of psychic events quite inaccessible to direct representation is a central theme of turn-of-the-century art. Simmel stated the problem thus: 'I am . . . convinced that the human individual does not end, as it were, at the frontiers marked by our senses of sight and touch, but that there exists another sphere, above and beyond—whether we think of it as something substantial or as some form of radiation—the extent of which is beyond all hypothesis, and which is just as much part of the person as the visible and tangible body.'[16]

In the 1890s Edvard Munch—whom Kokoschka always revered—had often shown his figures surrounded by emanations, whether coloured veils or streaming lines of force. For Vasily Kandinsky, around 1910, the aura as defined by the Theosophists became the literal vehicle of his art.[17] The figure in *Lady in Moscow* (fig. 5), for instance, is shrouded in a coloured form that appears in a very similar way in Annie Besant's and C. W. Leadbeater's Theosophical classic, *Thought-Forms*, as the aura of health. This marks an important juncture in Kandinsky's artistic development, the inclusion of free-floating, 'non-objective' colour areas within the painting.

Kokoschka has no truck with explanatory connections of this sort. He defines the purpose of these portraits purely in negative terms: they are 'not concerned with the externals of a person'.[18] And so he builds up non-material fields of force around his figures. The head of Martha Hirsch (plate 3), described by Kurt Hiller in an exhibition review in 1910 as 'an unhappy woman, pale, nervous, care-worn, with her daemonic cow-eyes narrowed to a depressive slit',[19] exudes a dark shadow, like a chill wind. Lotte Franzos (plate 2) seems trapped within a broad, blue outline. In portraits of two sanatorium patients, Ludwig Ritter von Janikowski (plate 10) and Conte Verona (plate 11), as also in *Adolf Loos* (fig. 6) and *Auguste Forel* (fig. 7), Kokoschka detaches the emanations from the figures, so that the whole background seems infused with tension. Personal space is thus relieved of its anecdotal, illustrative character and made to define the image itself.

Hands are stressed as the vehicles of expression. Folded or superimposed hands are rare in the portraits painted between 1907 and 1914. They would have served to underscore a calm, collected, self-contained attitude; but of course that is not what is intended. Even where hands are folded, as in *Adolf Loos*, their form undermines the predictable expressive message of their position. Crudely fleshy and oversized, they interlock like a power coupling; in contrast to the sitter's weary-looking face, they form an autonomous zone of taut energy. This contradiction throws the whole pose out of balance.

Open hands, by contrast, directly suggest movement. Rudolf Blümner, actor, reciter and friend of Herwarth Walden, is caught in a pose of dramatic declamation (plate 13). Seen in isolation, the face might equally well be registering terror or horror, but the gesture of the right hand defines the rhetorical context. In the case of *Conte Verona*, by contrast, it remains an open question whether the sitter is speaking or—as seems more likely—has stopped short in mid-gesture.

This almost pantomimic movement of hands is already present in Kokoschka's illustrations to his own prose tale *Die träumenden Knaben* (The Dreaming Youths). The figures in *The Awakeners* (fig. 8), for instance, grope their way from sleep to waking with theatrical gestures that give visual effect to the transition. Mime and dance are the prototypical *fin de siècle* arts; wordlessly enacted, they are 'emanations of absolute sensuous beauty' that counter the ossified conventions of speech. For Hofmannsthal the body in motion, in mime or dance, is a perfect whole; it expresses the 'inner plenitude . . . of the soul'[20] that goes far beyond all utilitarian categories.

In Kokoschka's portraits, however, the aestheticized gestural language of the *fin de siècle* is transformed by a disjointed, overwrought quality. 'The forces of our psyche', wrote Marie Herzfeld, analysing the contemporary mood in 1893, 'do not work together toward a single point; they obey no central impulse but turn against each other.'[21]

The artistic consequences of this process are pointed out by Rainer Maria Rilke in his analysis of Rodin's sculptural

Fig. 6 *Adolf Loos*, 1909; oil on canvas, 74 x 91 cm.
Staatliche Museen Preussischer Kulturbesitz, Nationalgalerie, Berlin

Fig. 7 *Auguste Forel*, 1910; oil on canvas, 70 x 58 cm.
Städtische Kunsthalle, Mannheim

language of gesture: the gestures of modern human beings have an impatient, high-strung and also hesitant quality that distinguishes them from the straightforward, purposeful gestures of past generations. Between the beginning and the end 'countless transitions have intervened; and in these intermediate states contemporary man turns out to have spent his life'.[22]

Looking at the hands of Kokoschka's sitters, one becomes aware of a concentration on these states of transition. Auguste Forel absently tucks his thumb into his sleeve. Martha Hirsch crosses her arms at the wrists, as if manacled; in this fixed, unnatural position the fingers of the left hand are almost convulsively tensed, as if all her pent-up motive energy were concentrated there. With one hand Lotte Franzos seems on the point of launching into a gesture; the other hand clutches her dress. There is no telling which impulse will prevail.

A characteristic of these early portraits is the instability of the figures in pictorial space. In technical terms, this arises from the way the paint is applied.[23] A thin skin of paint, intermittently exposing the bare canvas beneath, alternates with passages of heavy, crusted impasto. Outlines suddenly break off or fade imperceptibly into the ground. Marks made by pins or finger-nails appear all over the figures, forming tiny craters or force-fields, as in *Rudolf Blümner*, or seeming to spurt out of the body, as in *Lotte Franzos*. In 1962 Kokoschka recalled that he had painted Lotte 'like a candle flame: yellow and transparent light blue inside, and, all about, an aura of vivid dark blue'.[24]

In other portraits, mostly dating from 1911/12, Kokoschka abandoned the use of such quasi-literal signs as emanations and auras. In these works not the figure alone but the whole pictorial space is destabilized. The portrait of

Karl Etlinger is built up almost like a landscape:[25] the face towers like a mountain massif above the clouded foothills of the hands. This stretching of space is particularly apparent in *Egon Wellesz* (plate 17). Against a nebulous background, the head is sharp and frontal; below, in the central area, figure and ground coalesce; the hands are back in focus. The shifting nature of human appearances is expressed in terms of pictorial space.

VI

Kokoschka told of a number of situations in his life in which his ability to orientate himself in space had suddenly deserted him. In July 1909, on his way home from the tumultuous premiere of his play *Mörder Hoffnung der Frauen* (Murderer Hope of Women), he had a moment of dislocation of consciousness:

> My shadow had separated itself from my legs, as if the ground beneath me had started to roll away, shadow and all . . . . The whole thing may have lasted a fraction of a second, as I flew upwards, as it were, struggling to bring my legs down again, and was forced to move my whole body until I was in a horizontal position, with my left side hanging down slightly. In water, or in any medium heavier than air, there would have been nothing absurd about this. Many years later, in the Great War, I suffered from a similar sensory illusion for a long time after being shot in the head, because the labyrinth in my left inner ear, the organ of balance, had been destroyed.[26]

The search for traces of this early experience in his work (or at least for signs of a predisposition to such experiences) leads us to the *catalogue raisonné* of his paintings. Down to 1915 this lists only five paintings in which the figures are not standing or seated, and none of these contains anything that could be described as a stable, horizontal, reclining pose. At

Fig. 8 *The Awakeners*, 1907; woodcut illustration
for *The Dreaming Youths*

first sight, the boy and girl in *Children Playing* of 1909 (plate 8) seem to have paused in their game to lie down on the floor. However, in the girl's case especially, the nature of their contact with that floor remains undefined—as, indeed, does the location of the floor itself. *Annunciation* of 1911 (plate 20) shows the moment when the Virgin starts up from her recumbent position; the floor in the right foreground surges in sympathy, like water. The portrait of the writer Albert Ehrenstein (plate 31) frames the sitter diagonally in the space, looking upwards from right to left and resting on nothing. All stabilizing axes, horizontal or vertical, have disappeared.

The Ehrenstein portrait was painted shortly before *The Tempest* (plate 25), in which the system of co-ordinates by which we customarily find our bearings in the world is totally abolished, and the whole of space is plunged into turmoil. This painting marks the end of Kokoschka's love affair with Alma Mahler. It shows the couple lying adrift on what Kokoschka called 'a wreck in the world-ocean'.[27] The boat is breaking up; its remains are barely distinguishable from the waves.

Knight Errant (plate 33), begun just before the outbreak of the First World War, can be seen as a sequel to *The Tempest*. The knight has Kokoschka's features, and the woman crawling in the background those of Alma Mahler. The couple have been separated and the knight floats in despair above a wasteland. *Knight Errant* marks the completion of the artistic metamorphosis that was set off when 'Kokoschka's premonitory hallucination of 1909 . . . irrevocably transformed his pictorial world. As he plunges and hovers, the traditional

perspectives topple and the old centre of perspectival space is left void. The seeing self is not a static focus where rays converge.'[28]

VII

The opening up of space through a specific form of spatial experience that transcends objectivized perspectival modes of perception links Kokoschka with the project undertaken by the hero of Robert Musil's novel *Der Mann ohne Eigenschaften* (The Man Without Qualities), who attempts to carve out a field of operation on the borderline between outer and inner experience. Ulrich, the Man Without Qualities, looks out from the palace of Count Leinsdorf at a passing demonstration; behind him,

> he felt the presence of the room.... And that in itself now had something of the quality of a little stage, on which he stood right out in front, in the opening between the curtains, while outside, on the greater stage, the drama went past; and these two stages had a peculiar way of uniting, without regard for the fact that he stood between them. Then the room as he knew it to be there behind his back, his impression and awareness of it, contracted and turned inside out, passing through him or flowing past him like something very soft and yielding all around him.... The people were moving along behind him, and he was being lapped by them like a stone lapped by the ever-changing, ever-constant ripples of a stream. It was an experience that was only half-comprehensible.[29]

In the course of the novel this leads on to the 'Other State', the mystical experiment conducted by Ulrich and his sister Agathe. There are theoretical influences here; one of them is mentioned by Ulrich himself after his reunion with Agathe, when he recalls the 'work of a psychologist' who distinguishes between two categories of mental sensation, that of being encompassed by the content of experiences and that of encompassing them—or that of being 'spatial' and that of being 'corporeal'—and wonders where the original connection between the two might lie.[30]

Here, Ulrich is referring to the essay 'Über optische Inversion' (On Optical Inversion, 1922) by the psychologist Erich M. von Hornbostel,[31] a friend of Musil's. Hornbostel takes as his point of departure the inversion of spatial structures, as practised since time immemorial by the makers of moulds and dies, but here enlisted to support a psychological theory of spatial perception. An example is a drawing of a cube in which the near and far surfaces change places according to the way we look at it; the only thing that is impossible is that we should see it both ways at once. In the third dimension the convex is closed and exclusive; it is an object. The convex, on the other hand, is a space, open and inclusive. To reverse this—and the same applies to experiences—is to make the convex concave, and vice versa; and so the view from without and the view from within (or, in other words, Abstraction and Empathy) alternate and interact.

Gestalt psychologists regarded this phenomenon as proof of the spontaneity of perceptual organization. Implicitly, however, Hornbostel's text reflects the emergence of a new sensitivity towards complex forms of spatial experience. On their different levels, Loos, Kokoschka and Musil all discredit one-sided attitudes.

Notes

The phrase used in the title of this essay, 'lurching space' (*wankender Raum*), is a quotation from Kokoschka's drama *Mörder Hoffnung der Frauen*.

1 Adolf Loos, 'Das Prinzip der Bekleidung', in idem, *Sämtliche Schriften*, ed. Franz Glück, 2 vols, Vienna, 1962, vol. 1, p. 105 f.

2 Oskar Kokoschka, *Schriften 1907-1955*, ed. Hans Maria Wingler, Munich, 1956, pp. 355, 353.

3 Albert Ehrenstein, 'Oskar Kokoschka', *Die literarische Gesellschaft* 3 (1917), pp. 311-14.

4 Max Dvořák, preface to the portfolio *Variationen über ein Thema*, repr. in Hans Maria Wingler and Friedrich Welz, *Oskar Kokoschka: Das Druckgraphische Werk*, Salzburg, 1975, pp. 40-2.

5 Immanuel Kant, *Dreams of a Spirit-Seer, Illustrated by Dreams of Metaphysics*, trans. Emanuel F. Goerwitz, London, 1900, p. 118.

6 Lecture published in Oskar Kokoschka, *Vom Erlebnis im Leben: Schriften und Bilder*, ed. Otto Breicha, Salzburg, 1976, p. 33.

7 Oskar Kokoschka, *My Life*, trans. David Britt, London and New York, 1974, p. 45 f.

8 Hugo von Hofmannsthal, 'The Letter of Lord Chandos', in idem, *Selected Prose*, trans. Mary Hottinger and Tania and James Stern, with an introduction by Hermann Broch, London, 1952, p. 134.

9 Alfred Kubin, *Die andere Seite* (1909), repr. Munich, 1975, p. 187.

10 Etching, 12 x 7.9 cm, inscribed 'Ensor' l. r.

11 See *Symbolismus in Europa*, exhibition catalogue, Baden-Baden, Staatliche Kunsthalle, 1976, p. 123 ff.

12 See J. D. Bernal, *Wissenschaft*, Reinbek, 1970, vol. 3, p. 680 ff.

13 Thomas Mann, *Der Zauberberg* (1924), Frankfurt, 1976, pp. 341, 1, 259 f., 245, 154.

14 Georg Simmel, 'Das Problem des Porträts', *Die Neue Rundschau* 29 (1918), pp. 1336-44, repr. in idem, *Zur Philosophie der Kunst*, Potsdam, 1922, pp. 96-109.

15 Idem, 'Die Grossstädte und das Geistesleben' (1903), in idem, *Brücke und Tür*, Stuttgart, 1957, p. 228, and *Soziologie* (1908), Berlin, 1958, p. 15.

16 Idem, *Fragmente und Aufsätze aus dem Nachlass*, Munich, 1923, p. 174 f.

17 Sixten Ringbom, 'Kandinsky und das Okkulte', in *Kandinsky und München*, exhibition catalogue, Munich, Städtische Galerie im Lenbachhaus, 1982, p. 94 f.

18 Kokoschka, *My Life*, p. 33.

19 Kurt Hiller, 'Oskar Kokoschka', *Der Sturm* 1 (1910), p. 150.

20 Hugo von Hofmannsthal, 'Die unvergleichliche Tänzerin' (1906) and 'Über die Pantomime' (1911), in idem, *Reden und Aufsätze*, Frankfurt, 1979, vol. 1, pp. 499 f., 505.

21 Quoted in *Die Wiener Moderne*, ed. Gotthard Wunberg, Stuttgart, 1981, p. 260 f.

22 Rainer Maria Rilke, *Auguste Rodin*, Frankfurt, 1984, p. 37 f.

23 See Fritz Schmalenbach, *Oskar Kokoschka*, Königstein im Taunus, 1967, p. 6 ff.

24 Quoted in Ludwig Goldscheider, *Kokoschka*, London, 1963, p. 14.

25 *Karl Etlinger*, 1912; oil on canvas, 68 x 56 cm; inscribed 'OK' l. r.; Staatliche Kunstsammlungen, Karlsruhe.

26 Oskar Kokoschka, 'Vom Erleben' (1935), in *Vom Erlebnis im Leben*, p. 136; see also Kokoschka, *My Life*, pp. 68 f., 30 f.

27 Oskar Kokoschka, 'Trakl zu Besuch' (1915), in *Vom Erlebnis im Leben*, p. 80.

28 Jeannot Simmen, 'Oskar Kokoschka: Todes-Erfahrung und Schwebe-Halluzination', in idem, *Vertigo*, Munich, 1990, pp. 115-36 (this quotation, p. 132).

29 Robert Musil, *The Man Without Qualities*, trans. Eithne Wilkins and Ernst Kaiser, London, 1979, vol. 2, p. 412.

30 Ibid., vol. 3, p. 23.

31 Erich M. von Hornbostel, 'Über optische Inversion', *Psychologische Forschung* 1 (1922), p. 130 ff., especially p. 151 ff.

Ingried Brugger

Being at Odds with Being

Work in Dresden, 1916-1923

Given the thematic and stylistic variety of the work produced by Kokoschka between 1916 and 1923, it may seem surprising that it has come to be seen as more of a coherent unit than any other group in his *oeuvre*. This unique position of the Dresden work is not explained by any *genius loci* but by the artist's life at that time—which, in turn, reveals a complexity, a tissue of contradictions and self-doubts, that seems out of keeping with the homogeneity of his creative process.

*'How is it that some people live in Biarritz
and I live in Saxony?'*[1]

In late 1922 and early 1923 Kokoschka painted *Self-Portrait with Crossed Arms*, in which his gaze is directed both inwards and at the viewer (plate 50). His sceptical, even brooding expression evokes the precarious state of his life in Dresden; the position of the arms demonstrates containment, enclosure, introversion. Soon after it was painted, Kokoschka left Dresden, where he had taken refuge in 1916 after a serious war wound and the unhappy ending of his affair with Alma Mahler. Like Prague in later years, the Saxon capital was a place of refuge, albeit in this case always an unloved one. He noted in November 1919: 'And I carry so much in my heart, and here it will all remain unborn; here, where I am forced to live oppressed and disfigured by care and anxiety, without the sun, which I worship, without vitality and without the joy of love, which comes too naturally to me for me to let it be perverted in such a sorry, Saxon world.'[2] His letters from Dresden invariably speak of his dream of leaving the city, of travelling, of going somewhere where 'it is really hot', because he 'can bear this Germany no longer'.[3]

Oskar Kokoschka's Dresden 'debut' was in 1914, when he exhibited at the 'Expressionist Exhibition' as 'one of the rare spiritual personalities of Austro-German Expressionism'.[4] Locally, despite some adverse criticism, the exhibition at the Galerie Arnold not only rehabilitated the artists of the *Brücke* group, who had moved away from Dresden, but secured the recognition of Expressionism in general.[5] It made Kokoschka known in Dresden as a leading painter of new ideas.

The Dresden years brought Kokoschka recognition and success,[6] but they were marked by deep depression in his personal life. The inner context of that depression was made visible retrospectively in *The Tempest* (plate 25), in *Still Life with Putto and Rabbit* (plate 30), in *The Power of Music* (plate 42) and in the subsequent doll paintings, such as *Self-Portrait at the Easel* (plate 49). In his work he was trying to get over the loss of Alma Mahler, and later to overcome his own crippling rejection of contact with the world around him.[7]

It is an illuminating sidelight on Kokoschka's attitude to art and politics that in 1920, as a professor at the Dresden academy, he spoke out against the destruction of the artistic heritage by armed bands of revolutionaries. Prompted by the damaging of a Rubens painting in the Zwinger in an exchange of fire during the Kapp-Putsch, his protest appeared in over forty German daily papers and was posted all over the city of Dresden itself. It led to a quarrel with the revolutionary Communist artists George Grosz and John Heartfield, who publicly called him an 'Art Thug' (*Kunstlump*). To them he was a traitor, and they saw his manifesto —which described works of art as the 'most sacred assets' of the German people, which no party 'whether of the radical left, the radical right or the radical centre' had any right to endanger by firing a shot anywhere near a museum—as an insidious bourgeois attempt to undermine the class struggle. To Communist artists the non-realist art of Expressionism was the art of the bourgeoisie, and the Weimar Republic was the acme of the bourgeois state.

Kokoschka and German Expressionism

Kokoschka's plea for the unique value of art belongs to a humanistic tradition. It is also symptomatic of the divided state of German Expressionism in the immediate aftermath of the First World War.[8] The *Brücke* group, founded in Dresden in 1905 and subsequently (from 1911) based in Berlin, had dissolved in 1913 over internal disagreements. The Munich group *Der Blaue Reiter*, led by Vasily Kandinsky and Franz Marc, had disintegrated in 1914. After the end of the First World War there began in Germany a new and intensive burst of artistic activity, which emerged mainly in the wake of the November Revolution of 1918.[9] The Dresden Secession, formed in 1919, and the *Arbeitsrat für Kunst* (Workers' Council for Art) and the *Novembergruppe*, both in Berlin, were radical associations of artists, mainly led by Communist activists.

For artists of that generation in Dresden, Berlin and Munich the break with bourgeois art was irrevocable. In their pursuit of a 'new human being' and a 'new society' they added a political dimension to their art. Their demand for more hard truths in art (*Verismus*) led them to inject social criticism into their subject-matter and to seek new stylistic and formal solutions that led away from Expressionism, with its subjectivity, gestural style and delight in colour.

A comparison with the artists who were working in Dresden and Berlin at the time—for example, Otto Dix, Conrad Felixmüller and George Grosz—shows in itself how little

Fig. 1   George Grosz, *Metropolis*, 1916/17; oil on canvas, 100 x 102 cm.
Thyssen-Bornemisza Collection, Lugano

Kokoschka was affected in his art by such social calamities in
Dresden during the Weimar Republic as the impoverish-
ment of the proletariat or the misery of war veterans. Grosz,
in his *Metropolis* (1916/17; fig. 1), takes a close look at the
'dregs of society', beggars, whores, cripples and profiteers;
by comparison with that great vortex of urban chaos and
misery, Kokoschka's Dresden views (see fig. 3) look like
antidotes to a bleak reality, showing the still-intact city at a
safe distance from its workaday self. Felixmüller, in images
such as *The Ruhr District* of 1920,[10] brings the sufferings of the
exploited working population uncompromisingly into focus;
Walter Jacob, in *Last Judgment*, also of 1920 (fig. 2), gives an
apocalyptic vision of society. By contrast, the figure compositions that Kokoschka painted in Dresden are caught up
in a field of force made up of personal relationships and
conflicts; these are sensitive images of character, in which
the individual is subjected to a concentrated analysis of his
or her personality.

It is this reversion to the individual that marks the fundamental divide between Kokoschka and German Expressionism, as represented not only by Expressionistic *Verismus*, but
also by the *Brücke* artists: Kokoschka differs as much from
Ernst Ludwig Kirchner or Karl Schmidt-Rottluff as he does
from Dix and Grosz. Werner Hofmann has pointed out how
deeply Kokoschka, with his tendency to 'sacrifice the general, the typical and the symptomatic to the individual and,
ultimately, to the most intensely subjective feeling', is in-
debted to the Austrian tradition: one has only to think of
Richard Gerstl and Egon Schiele.[11]

Colour and Space

Herwarth Walden's expanded concept of Expressionism,
which aimed at a synthesis of Expressionist gestural form
with Futurism and Cubism, became the credo of a section of
the German avant-garde. The interlocking of stylistic devices
vividly exemplified by Dix's *Leda* of 1919 (fig. 4) and by
Felixmüller's *Portrait of Felix Stiemer*[12] goes to show how
strongly Kokoschka was setting himself apart from his contemporaries in formal as well as in other terms.

It has become customary to isolate Kokoschka's Dresden
works from the rest of his *oeuvre* as a phase of 'colour painting' pure and simple, in which he eliminated 'all previously
developed forms of linearity'[13] and moved closer to the
painting of the *Brücke* artists, and to that of Emil Nolde in
particular. However, the first characteristic example of this
style, *The Power of Music* (plate 42), was not created until
1920; conversely, as early as 1923, in *Dresden, Augustus
Bridge with Steamer I* (plate 45), we find a stylistic anticipation of the landscapes and townscapes painted during his
later years of travel.

By 1916, in such works as the portrait of Princess Mechtilde Lichnowsky (plate 34) or *Lady with Parrot* (plate 36),
the distinct artistic resources of 'line' and 'colour' begin to
coalesce.[14] Colour, still restricted to the visible brushstroke,
becomes the vehicle of expression. With this goes both a
thickening of the paint, which is applied with a heavier impasto, and an abstraction of the brushstrokes into eloquent,
symbolic abbreviations. The painted surface thus takes on a
unified quality, and the objects in the picture cohere opti-
cally. Characteristic examples are *The Friends* (fig. 8) and
Lovers with Cat (plate 37).

Fig. 2   Walter Jacob, *Last Judgment,* 1920; oil on canvas,
115.3 x 120.7 cm. The Robert Gore Rifkind Foundation,
Beverly Hills

Fig. 3 *Dresden, Neustadt IV*, 1921; oil on canvas, 68.5 x 109.2 cm. Private collection

A certain 'dirtying' of the colour in 1918 and 1919—as in *Self-Portrait, Hand to Mouth* (plate 41)—was countered, a year later, by the intense, glowing, primary colour chords of *The Power of Music*, in which rhythmic, linear brushwork welds itself into impasto slabs of colour. In the spring of 1920 Kokoschka wrote: 'I am trying, with some success, to bring off the feat...of remaining absolutely courageous, joyous and youthful...and not being pinned down anywhere but in my paintings; this year one of them at least will be such that nothing more joyous and glowing could possibly be imagined, unless one were to paint with rockets.'[15] He painted pictures whose radiance obliterated his oppressive surroundings. Not even the ugly distortion of the facial features can take away the cheerful, almost idyllic air of *Child with Flowers and Cat* (fig. 5) or *Summer I*.[16]

Beginning with patches of colour in varying sizes and configurations, which seem to hover weightlessly over the picture plane, Kokoschka goes on to create increasingly abstract, intrinsically static, internally homogeneous areas of colour with an ever-greater tactile character. In addition, the application of colour in blocks begins to fall into a basic rectangular pattern. Planes in horizontal and vertical alignment, but no longer necessarily coinciding with the silhouettes of the objects, are directly butted against each other; passages of darkness run across the entire surface of the picture. The lighting is full of contrasts. Colour behaves like matter; planes of shade butt on to areas of light; spatial structures emerge.

This is strikingly exemplified by *Dresden, the Elbe Bridges (with Figure from Behind)* of 1923 (fig. 6) and by *Self-Portrait with Crossed Arms* (plate 50). Viewed from a distance, these works generate an illusion which, strictly speaking, the actual construction of the surface, built up from 'planar' areas of colour, contradicts.

In 1923 Kokoschka painted a Dresden view very different from his previous ones. In *Dresden, Augustus Bridge with Steamer I* (plate 45) the colour is less heavily weighted and the blocks of paint give way to a handling that communicates excitement and animation, inner unrest, pulsating life. Line becomes the principal source of spatial struc-

Fig. 4 Otto Dix, *Leda*, 1919; oil on canvas, 103.5 x 80.5 cm. Los Angeles County Museum of Art

ture. The large motifs, such as bridges or river banks, are no longer placed parallel to the picture plane but recede along diagonals that suggest depth.

Kokoschka's Dresden work thus marks a vital turning-point in his stylistic evolution. The 'mature' Dresden style, first seen in *The Power of Music* and culminating in *Self-Portrait with Crossed Arms*, had sprung from systematic preparatory work that went back to 1916; and it was while he was still in Dresden that Kokoschka evolved the pictorial conception that was to characterize his years of travel, in which he returned to linear form and thin, transparent paint, but united in a synthesis with the spatial power achieved in Dresden.

Individual and Group

'Exiles: these are people whom the barbarity of our age has made into restless nomads, and who have no home, because in the clutches of brute force the mind feels uprooted; people hounded away from their true human work, whose only

Fig. 5 *Child with Flowers and Cat*, 1920; oil on canvas, 127.6 x 81 cm. Bayerische Staatsgemäldesammlungen, Staatsgalerie moderner Kunst, Munich

recourse is to find a new home in the soul.'[17] The words are those of Paul Westheim, describing a painting that Kokoschka began in 1916 and completed early in 1917: *The Exiles* (fig. 7). This was Kokoschka's first true group picture. The sitters are the actress Käthe Richter, with whom Kokoschka had become friendly during his stay in the Weisser Hirsch Sanatorium, near Dresden; the physician Dr. Fritz Neuburger; and the artist himself.

'Each of the earlier portraits was the product of a personal confrontation between artist and sitter.... Now, without losing any of their force and tension, the individual identities are linked together; the mental current completes its circuit inside the picture itself, and the creation has released itself more firmly from its creator; it has become more capable of independent life.'[18] Thus the art historian Hans Tietze described Kokoschka's new relationship with the human image, as manifested in the group portraits of the early Dresden years. The sitters have become a group, mentally, by virtue of their common status as 'exiles'. Each of them retains the freedom to take his or her own decisions, and so the dialogue between the individual and the group remains inconclusive: the individual is continually summoned to interaction. Kokoschka has conceived the group as a dynamic whole, albeit a whole that is impermanent and subject to change.

In his early portraits Kokoschka had torn the mask of status from the face of the bourgeois individual, stripping the psyche bare; in the group portraits, again, what interested him was the unique physiognomy, the individual fate. Thus, in *The Friends* (fig. 8) the game of cards played by Kokoschka's Dresden friends of 1917/18 reveals a panorama of strongly differentiated manners and possibilities of individual action. Kokoschka himself wrote of this painting: 'My friends are in it, playing cards. Each one in his passion terribly naked, and all drenched in colour of a higher order which binds them together as light does an object and raises its mirrored image into a category having something of reality and something of the mirrored image and therefore more of both.'[19]

The artist's touch hauntingly refracts the images of his friends' personalities through divergent, seemingly immaterial colour, animated structure and a nervous brushstroke that lends uneven accents to their bodies. To the individual the game becomes a psychic and social revelation in which he perceives himself as an 'acting self'[20] and at the same time confirms his collective identity. By using the shared activity of cards to detach the individual from his own purpose in life, Kokoschka carries that individual over into a more comprehensive vision of human existence.

These group pictures were followed, in 1920, by *The Power of Music* (plate 42), which Kokoschka was to regard as one of his major works. It marks the point at which he wrenched his work free from the 'private sphere of subjective expectations' and opened up the dimension of allegory, the coded message. In it he abandons the compositional rule of convergence. The two figures—the woman with the trumpet and the startled boy—are pulling apart and seem to refuse

Fig. 6 *Dresden, the Elbe Bridges (with Figure from Behind)*, 1923; oil on canvas, 65 x 90 cm.
Museum Folkwang, Essen

to communicate. Werner Hofmann interprets the way in which the boy turns away, overcome by the power of music, as a symptom of shock on an exalted plane: 'The original title [*Strength and Weakness*] made the partners into a pair of opposites; but ultimately that balance is reversed, and the weaker, though overcome, is strengthened.... Pointing beyond the pictorial space without in any way disowning the internal structure of the painting, the boy who is in the grip of music conveys that he is the victim of an explosive spiritual force that triumphantly transcends and supersedes traditional pictorial composition'.[21] And so a new, active element enters the structure of the work: its composition takes on an open, flowing, even overflowing aspect, thus anticipating an essential feature of Kokoschka's allegories of the 1930s and 1940s.

Couples: Love and Conflict

In the year in which Kokoschka painted his vision of exile he gave that work a moving pendant: the figure of Orpheus returning home. Here Eurydice kills Orpheus: man meets his end in the lap of woman and returns whence he came. Kokoschka interpreted the Orpheus and Eurydice legend on a number of levels: in 1917 he produced a drawing and the painting *Orpheus and Eurydice* (plate 38), and a year later completed a play with the same title.[22]

The connections are evident between Kokoschka's personal life, the close-up view he enjoyed in Dresden of the collapse of Kaiser Wilhelm's Germany, and his play. This is a drama of love; its action turns upon the horrors of war and the corruption of humankind. It is dominated by an oppres-

Fig. 7 *The Exiles*, 1916/17; oil on canvas, 94 x 145 cm.
Bayerische Staatsgemäldesammlungen, Staatsgalerie moderner Kunst,
Sammlung Fohn, Munich

Fig. 8 *The Friends*, 1917/18; oil on canvas, 100 x 150 cm. Neue Galerie der Stadt Linz

sive sense of finality: 'Beggars on crutches scatter scraps from a sack, around which fat, lazy persons quarrel as they wait in line to eat; lunatics try to climb the walls but slither down. Murderers with daggers pounce on his [Orpheus'] shadow. Lovers crawl away on all fours at his approach, clustering like a swarm of bees. Some have animal faces, or tails and claws; from within come titters, murmurs and shrieks of laughter.'

It is a finality to which Orpheus, in his last, mad cry, has no answer but the humanist commandment: Thou shalt not kill. Kokoschka always experienced 'unbridled chaos' as a direct and daemonic threat to himself, and regarded art as an act of self-defence: 'Once humanized by the imposition of artistic form, the unfathomable becomes imaginable and loses its terrors'.[23]

The subject of the painting is the threat posed by female sensuality. As in the paintings *Lovers with Cat* (plate 37) and *The Slave Girl* (fig. 10), both of which also take the vexed problem of sexual relations as their theme, the woman is isolated from the man and withdrawn into herself. She is clothed and seems to look within, while he, naked, turns yearning eyes on her. Orpheus has sought to use the power of the spirit, and of his art, to snatch Eurydice from Hades; and he loses her under the spell of his own sexual desires. Oblivious to the lyre that he holds at his side, he is also a failure as an artist. The opening in the background, emphasized by a thick black line, separates the man and the woman both in the formal sense and in its capacity as the gate of Hades.

The conflict between the sexes, as presented here by Kokoschka, also refers to the artist's love affair with Alma Mahler, which had come to an end in 1914. In 1918 he commissioned a puppet-maker in Munich, Hermine Moos, to make him a life-size replica of Alma's body as a substitute for the lost contact with his beloved.[24] On completion, this highly unsatisfactory surrogate (fig. 14, p. 217), this 'shoddy

doll-fetish', as he himself later called it dismissively, turned out to be a hollow mockery of any erotic magic he might have hoped for. It was thereupon converted into a still-life object. Numerous drawings and a number of paintings revolve around that failed doll; it was in his art that Alma's symbolic *Ersatz* came alive.

His gradual attainment of an ironic detachment from the doll fetish, as expressed in his work between 1919 and 1922, reached its conclusion in *Self-Portrait at the Easel* of 1922 (plate 49). In *Woman in Blue* of 1919 (fig. 9) Kokoschka had transformed the doll into a hybrid entity between puppet and person; by 1922, in *Self-Portrait with Doll* (fig. 11), he was stylizing his own form into a lay figure: an artist's anatomical teaching aid. In *Self-Portrait at the Easel* the doll is reduced to a lifeless piece of matter, a grotesque parody of what had once been a surrogate body. The artist's own self-portrait has elements of caricature. He stares out of the picture with unseeing eyes, lost in a tactile exploration of the doll's lifeless body, which he paints as if in a trance. In this painting Kokoschka was able to mock his own obsession with the doll and the fetishism that had transformed it into his model. And as he did so, both were overcome.

Images of the Ego: The Dresden Self-Portraits

The unsuccessful attempt to take 'refuge' in the doll was an important episode in Kokoschka's life. In those paintings in which the artist shows himself and the doll together, the choice of himself as a theme is closely tied to personal experience and to personal problems. The form of representation emphasizes a situation, a finite moment in time: the artist-sitter and his doll are engaged in a transaction. In *Self-Portrait at the Easel* he goes further, and specifies the place: in the background is the window of his Dresden studio, with a view over Neustadt to the bank of the Elbe.

Fig. 9 *Woman in Blue*, 1919; oil on canvas, 75 x 100 cm. Staatsgalerie, Stuttgart

Kokoschka adopts a quite different approach in *Self-Portrait, Hand to Mouth* of 1918/19 (plate 41) and in *Self-Portrait with Crossed Arms* of four years later (plate 50). With a sparing use of signs—hand raised to lips, questioning stare, unstable posture, head tilted back in the earlier painting; arms folded, doubtfully introverted gaze, squarely set torso, head slightly turned in the later one—the artist-sitter indicates forms of personal relevance that transcend the immediate situation. He asserts an identity that persists beyond the Here and Now, whether as its continuation or as its negation. The self in these portraits involves itself in the sufferings of the age, which it faces with scepticism, doubt and disquiet. However, the vulnerability, loneliness and *Angst* that emerge from these works also emphasize the artist's unconditional acceptance of the conflicts that assail him.

After comporting himself in his early Vienna years as a 'savage chieftain'[25] and a social outsider—with shaven head and lofty scorn for the smug self-satisfaction of the bourgeoisie—the painter initially found in Dresden, too, that his unbourgeois life-style led people to call him 'crazy Kokoschka'. Numerous works, from *Design for 'Sturm' Poster* of 1910[26] to *Self-Portrait with Doll* and *Self-Portrait at the Easel*, supply evidence of this non-conformist role. This does seem rather at variance with his persistent—and ultimately, in 1919, successful—efforts to secure a professorship at the Dresden academy. It is a contradiction central to Kokoschka's whole life.

The quest for permanence and order runs through the artist's life. It emerges, for instance, in his unquestioning acceptance, over the years, of the self-imposed duty of providing for his own family; in his utopian insistence on demanding, both of himself and of Alma Mahler, an eternal and absolute love; and in all his efforts to gain recognition from the cultural Establishment.

This contradiction clearly emerges from the contrast between *Self-Portrait at the Easel* and *Self-Portrait with Crossed Arms*. Both are extreme manifestations of states of mind, and both show Kokoschka as a man inwardly torn. Of all the Dresden self-portraits, *Self-Portrait at the Easel* was the one he liked least. He called it 'The Cripple', and many years later he

Fig. 10 *The Slave Girl*, 1923; oil on canvas, 110.5 x 80 cm. The Saint Louis Art Museum

Fig. 11 *Self-Portrait with Doll*, 1922; oil on canvas, 84 x 119 cm.
Staatliche Museen Preussischer Kulturbesitz, Nationalgalerie, Berlin

made efforts to have it deleted from the *catalogue raisonné* of his works. Significantly, it remained unfinished; in it, Kokoschka had created a grotesquely deformed travesty of himself.

Self-Portrait with Crossed Arms, on the other hand, does full justice to the social status of an academy professor. The conventional suit, the dignified posture, the monumental structure of the portrait, with its low viewpoint, inherited from a long tradition of official portraiture, and the reserve conveyed by the face and by the position of the arms, give the artist—in spite of the body-language, with its message of doubt—a touch of self-importance.

It was not only stylistically that Dresden occupied a pivotal position between the 'early work' and the evolution of Kokoschka's art after 1924. In the Dresden years Kokoschka evolved the pictorial formulas that came to underlie all his later work: the concept of the *Weltlandschaft* (cosmic landscape), both urban and rural, and a new image of human beings, in double and group portraits, which he defined as early as 1917 in a letter to the art historian Hans Tietze: 'And so I am building up human faces into compositions; in them, being is at odds with being, in total opposition, like hatred and love. In every picture, I look for the dramatic attribute that welds individual spirits together into a higher order.'[27]

Notes

1 Oskar Kokoschka, *Briefe*, ed. Olda Kokoschka and Heinz Spielmann, vol. 2, *1919-1934*, Düsseldorf, 1985, p. 59.

2 Ibid., p. 7.

3 Ibid., p. 70.

4 Preface to *Die neue Malerei*, exhibition catalogue, Dresden, Galerie Ernst Arnold, 1914. Kokoschka was represented by two portraits of women, one of them *Lady in Red* of 1911.

5 The Dresden critic Richard Stiller wrote: 'In a very few years the vitality of the latest trend in art—which so perplexed the sceptics with its shifting impression of originality and derivativeness, profundity and contrivance, mixed with sheer attention-seeking—has become all the more strongly apparent'.

6 Major museums bought Kokoschka's works, his first one-man show, at Cassirer's in Berlin in 1918, was a success and the first monograph on his work, by Paul Westheim, was published the same year. In 1919 he was appointed a professor at the Dresden academy, and his plays were performed under distinguished directors, such as Max Reinhardt of the Kammerspiele in Munich.

7 See Peter Gorse, 'Kokoschka und die Puppe', in *Oskar Kokoschka: Symposion*, ed. Erika Patka, Salzburg and Vienna, 1986, pp. 187-203.

8 See Donald E. Gordon, *Expressionism: Art and Idea*, London, 1987, p. 122 ff.

9 On the post-war generation of German Expressionists, see Stephanie Barron, ed., *German Expressionism 1915-1925: The Second Generation*, Los Angeles and Munich, 1988.

10 Conrad Felixmüller, *Ruhrrevier*, 1920; oil on canvas, 80 x 65 cm; private collection, Berlin. Barron, *German Expressionism*, cat. 51.

11 Werner Hofmann, *Grundlagen zur modernen Kunst*, 2nd edn, Stuttgart, 1978, p. 216.

12 Conrad Felixmüller, *Bildnis Felix Stiemer*, 1918; oil on canvas, 60 x 45 cm; Staatliche Museen Preussischer Kulturbesitz, Nationalgalerie, Berlin. Barron, *German Expressionism*, cat. 44.

13 Fritz Schmalenbach, *Oskar Kokoschka*, Königstein im Taunus, 1967, p. 26.

14 The group of large male portraits completed a short time before, including *Carl Moll* (plate 28), *Franz Hauer* (plate 29) and *Albert Ehrenstein* (plate 31), is different, both in the grey or blue-grey monochrome effect and in the linear, striated brushstrokes that are applied like contours.

15 Kokoschka, *Briefe*, p. 14.

16 *Sommer I*, 1920; oil on canvas, 111 x 140 cm; inscribed 'OK 20' u. r.; Staatliche Museen Preussischer Kulturbesitz, Nationalgalerie, Berlin, on loan from private collection.

17 Paul Westheim, 'Der Maler Oskar Kokoschka', *Kunstblatt* (1917), p. 300.

18 Hans Tietze, 'Oskar Kokoschkas neue Werke', *Die bildenden Künste* 2, nos. 11/12 (1919), pp. 249-56 (this quotation, p. 252).

19 Quoted in Hans Maria Wingler, *Oskar Kokoschka: The Work of the Painter*, trans. Frank S. Budgen, London, 1958, p. 307.

20 Oskar Kokoschka, in *Oskar Kokoschka: Aus seinem Schaffen, 1909-1950*, exhibition catalogue, Munich, Haus der Kunst, 1950, unpaginated.

21 Werner Hofmann, 'Der irrende Ritter', in *Oskar Kokoschka: Symposion*, pp. 265-78.

22 On Kokoschka's handling of the Orpheus and Eurydice myth, see Hofmann, 'Der irrende Ritter', and Henry I. Schvey, *Oskar Kokoschka: The Painter as Playwright*, Detroit, 1982, p. 110 ff.

23 Oskar Kokoschka, *My Life*, trans. David Britt, London and New York, 1974.

24 See Gorse, 'Kokoschka und die Puppe'.

25 This epithet (*Oberwildling*), which directly inspired the legend of Kokoschka as an 'unappreciated genius', was coined by Ludwig Hevesi on the occasion of the 1908 'Kunstschau' exhibition in Vienna.

26 *Entwurf zum Sturm-Plakat*, 1910; oil on canvas, 102 x 70 cm; inscribed 'OK' l. r.; Szépmüvészeti Múzeum, Budapest. The painting is a sketch for the 1910 poster for *Der Sturm*. The poster was initially used to advertise the magazine's first issue; in later use it was overprinted with the words 'Neue Nummer' (New Number). Kokoschka used the same subject in 1911/12 for a poster advertising a talk that he gave at the Akademischer Verband in Vienna.

27 Quoted in Tietze, 'Kokoschkas neue Werke', p. 251.

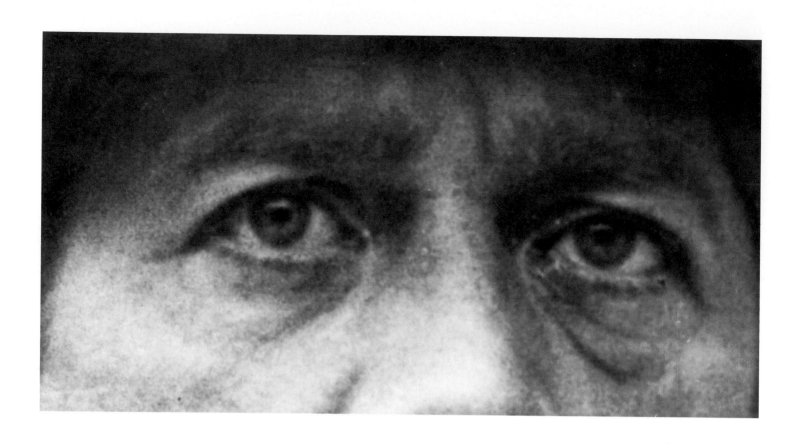

Edwin Lachnit

'Man Has Two Eyes'

The City Views

In 1923 Kokoschka broke away from the regular existence of an academy professor in Dresden and took to the road, like the journeymen in the craft guilds of old. Legend has it that he slipped away from the academy without telling a soul, simply calling out a good-bye to the doorman. What really happened was that on 8 September he applied to the Saxon Interior Ministry for two years' travel leave, which was granted on 24 September. He did not, however, return to his post after the two years had expired, so that eventually, in 1927, the faculty decided to appoint another professor, 'since it seems impossible to secure binding consent from Kokoschka'.[1] The name of his successor, incidentally, was Otto Dix.

Kokoschka first went to Vienna, and after his father's death in October 1923 he stayed there for a time with his family. In the spring of 1924 he travelled to Italy, visiting Venice and Florence. That autumn, with Adolf Loos and a fellow painter, Sebastian Isepp (a member of the Nötsch Group), he went to Paris, where he stayed for several weeks but was rather alienated by the eager bustle of the 'metropolis of art'.

Early in 1925 Kokoschka had a stroke of good fortune that was to have a decisive influence on his later life and career. The Berlin dealer Paul Cassirer, a notable patron of Kokoschka's work since 1910 or thereabouts, granted him an unlimited credit account for travel throughout Europe. The monies advanced were to be repaid from the sale of the resulting paintings.

The five years that followed were marked by a restless nomadism that took him all over the Continent and 'as far as the limits of the ancient Roman Empire': from the British Isles to North Africa and into the Near East. In 1925 he was in the South of France, Spain, Portugal and Holland; in 1926 in northern Germany and London; in 1927 in Berlin, Venice and the French Alps; in 1928 in Tunisia and Algeria; in 1929 in Cairo, Jerusalem, Damascus, Athens, Istanbul, Venice, Zurich and Scotland; in 1930 once more in North Africa and Italy—and that is only the most cursory outline of Kokoschka's itinerary.

The urge to travel was accompanied by an equally strong impulse to create. With the same implacable determination with which the tourist records, through the camera lens,

Fig. 1 *Dresden, Augustus Bridge with Steamer II*, 1923; oil on canvas, 65 x 95.5 cm.
Stedelijk Van Abbemuseum, Eindhoven

every stage of his journey, Kokoschka did so subjectively, with his brush. He painted views of all the places where he stayed: a vast cycle of townscapes that is unique in twentieth-century art. The analogy with a camera-toting holidaymaker is faulty, of course: the 'picturesque motif' of countless souvenir photographs was precisely what Kokoschka was not looking for.

The city as a subject remained important in Kokoschka's work from the Dresden years onwards. After the prelude of *Stockholm Harbor* of 1917 (plate 34) he went on between 1919 and 1923 to paint a series of views of the Elbe in Dresden, looking towards Neustadt (plates 43, 44) or the Augustus Bridge (plate 45; fig. 1). These reproduce the view from Kokoschka's studio window at the academy (see plate 49) and their composition is, in a sense, 'realistic'. The river, the skyline of the opposite bank and the sky are superimposed in horizontal bands—just as an observer would have perceived the scene in reality. However, this strictly horizontal structure is sometimes deliberately exaggerated—as when, for example, the bridge across the river, which ought to supply a line providing perspectival depth, is shifted to a horizontal position and coalesces with the opposite bank. Likewise, in the painting in which a visible observer is looking along the river (fig. 6, p. 23), the bridges supply the dominant direction, draw the two banks into the frontal view and shut off the space in the distance.

Fig. 2 Albrecht Altdorfer, *The Battle of Issus*, 1529; panel, 158 x 120 cm. Alte Pinakothek, Munich

Bipolar Perspective versus Classical Linear Perspective

Kokoschka's farewell to Dresden brought with it a radical compositional change. It was as if the abandonment of the static studio vantage-point, and the constant changes of scene, had transformed his habits of seeing and consequently his approach to pictorial structure. From now on Kokoschka consistently chose to work from a high viewpoint—such as a tower, an observation platform or a room on the top floor of a hotel—from which he could look both downwards and far into the distance. Bounded by a high horizon line, the urban panorama assumes a closed, elliptical form that encompasses extremes of breadth and of depth. The artist himself ascribed this preference for a bird's-eye view to his experiences in the trenches in the First World War: 'I wanted to escape from the filthy existence that they call a war, and I swore to myself: if I ever get out of this alive, and can paint again, I'm only ever going to stand and look out from the highest buildings or from mountains, right on the top, and see what goes on in cities and what happens to the people who live their miserable lives in those cities. And I have kept to it: my landscapes and townscapes are always painted from the very top'.[2]

As a sidelight on the artist's psychology this anecdotal statement is undoubtedly of interest, but it does little to further art historical analysis. Rather more promising clues are furnished by the explanations given by the artist in campaigning for his own 'bifocal perspective' against classical linear perspective: 'In contrast to Turner, who was a colourist in the tradition of the later Rubens, my landscapes are three-dimensional, painted spatially, based on an elliptical composition with two foci. Because I have always denounced the so-called *perspective cavalière*, with its single focus. Man has two eyes'.[3]

This bipolar form of composition makes it possible to accommodate a wider segment of reality on the canvas than the natural visual angle would permit.[4] The city appears not as an individualized topographical view, or *veduta*, but as an ideal macrocosm, analogous to the 'cosmic landscapes' of the sixteenth century. Kokoschka was susceptible to the fascination of the universal vision of Albrecht Altdorfer, to whose *The Battle of Issus* (fig. 2) he was later to pay tribute in an essay.[5]

Such a mode of vision has nothing in common with the optical phenomenalism of Impressionism, to which Kokoschka's townscapes are continually likened. Stylistically, it is true, the broad, impasto colour planes of the Dresden period gave way in the mid-1920s to a minute, vibrant handling in which the individual brushstroke or dab of colour assumed greater autonomy. The comparison with the atmospheric, flickering sensory response of Impressionism is, however, a purely superficial one. Kokoschka directs the instrument of the seeing eye towards no less an epistemological problem than:

What is reality? To think that Altdorfer could ever have been dismissed as a minor master of humanist historicism! That *The Battle of Issus* was not rather recognized as the first Baroque painting! This has come to be seen only now that two world wars have razed

Fig. 3 Rembrandt, *Stormy Landscape, with an Arched Bridge*, before 1638; panel, 28 x 40 cm.
Staatliche Museen Preussischer Kulturbesitz, Gemäldegalerie, Berlin

important centres of Baroque art to the ground. A whole chapter in the history of the West has been saved with Altdorfer's painting. *Eppure si muove*; the earth does revolve in this picture, which was painted before Galileo explained the nature of its motion. The spin is instantly perceptible: the spin of the blazing sunlight, space wheeling with the earth, pregnant with all that reality brings into the world.

More than a hundred years after this was painted, beings in human form would venture out into those expanses of space; and Christian saints and Olympian gods would cascade into cathedral and palace interiors out of the painted skies of the Baroque.[6]

Tracing the Baroque reference further, we find in the view of Lyons, painted in 1927 (plate 55), a successor to the Baroque landscape compositions of Adam Elsheimer, say, or Rembrandt (see fig. 3). Wedge-like, a gentle ridge slides in from one side and blends into the measureless expanse of a plain that draws the eye into unfathomed remoteness, dissolves the horizon and loses itself in the infinity of the sky. Like the elliptical panorama—and far more than the 'strip compositions' that were restricted to the Dresden period—

Fig. 4 *Madrid, Plaza Cánovas del Castillo*, 1925; oil on canvas, 67 x 98 cm.
Galerie Fischer, Lucerne

Fig. 5 *Jerusalem*, 1929; oil on canvas, 80 x 129 cm. The Detroit Institute of Arts

Kokoschka's 'Baroque' view of Lyons established a compositional formula that was to reappear again and again in his townscapes (see plate 72).

The Revelation of Energy Flow

Kokoschka's choice of a Baroque form of pictorial organization may not only be deduced from the visible result but also explained in terms of the underlying artistic intention. What

Otto Pächt said of Rembrandt's landscapes is equally true of Kokoschka's attitude to urban structure: 'Previously, every detail was referred to the observer's viewpoint, but now an even stronger unifying point of reference emerges: the unique and unrepeatable quality of subjective experience. We do not learn from Rembrandt what this landscape looks like in what might be called its normal state: it exists only as an inner experience that is conveyed to us subjectively, like a vision. His image of landscape is more than a mere optical experience: it is both nature and inner world'.[7]

Fig. 6 *Linz, View from the Pfenningberg*, 1955; oil on canvas, 88 x 116 cm.
Neue Galerie, Linz

Fig. 7 *Vienna, View from the Wilhelminenberg*, 1931; oil on canvas, 92 x 134 cm.
Historisches Museum der Stadt Wien, Vienna

What Kokoschka depicts is not individual physiognomy, not the topographical portrait of a specific city: here, as in his portraits of people, he has penetrated beyond the surface of sensory perception into the mental world that transforms matter into life. The city reveals itself to him—and he it to us—as a vital organism, pervaded by currents of energy, pulsating, dynamic, bursting the bounds of the two-dimensional picture plane (see fig. 4).

The point is driven home by a number of other things that Kokoschka says in his essay on Altdorfer:

The painter does not employ the single-focus perspective that was already becoming fashionable in Italy and in Flanders in his day. Ever since the Renaissance this so-called vanishing-point perspective has served painters as a crutch, enabling them to assign every figure to its allotted place at intervals determined by criteria of social status, with the aid of an artificial perspective, a theoretical depth and distance....

I should like to describe *The Battle of Issus* as a work of absolute painting. It grips you, as if the curtain had been drawn back to reveal not a mere peep-show stage but abyssal depths! The other side of reality is laid bare: not a transcendental side but one that can never be seen except by one who has learned inward vision. One is

Fig. 8 *Rome, Forum Romanum*, 1949; oil on canvas, 75 x 105 cm.
Private collection, Italy

Fig. 9 *Florence Cathedral*, 1948; oil on canvas, 96 x 126 cm.
The Minneapolis Institute of Arts

stunned by the power of this picture, which remodels the beholder's own visual imagination and remains active within it ever after; thanks to the surging, the overflowing, the damming and clenching of matter itself, the growing and burgeoning of vegetation, the roar of the waters, the clash and spring of rock and stone, the atmospheric cyclone of tension and discharge, all as if in response to some cataclysmic whim of nature herself.

Once stripped of all that words can express—what is nowadays called 'subject-matter'—the composition starts to take on a life of its own and to become form. Over all this lies a harmony that is no longer the harmony of those great painters from Van Eyck to Titian in whose work Divine Majesty has allowed the act of Creation to be repeated. Here matter becomes form, *Gestalt* .... In this work, as in a fugue, something is struggling to become form, and yet it is generated by absolute seeing and it opens up realms of reality quite different from those revealed by the inspired painters I just mentioned. The *passage of time*, in which the competing motifs of a musical fugue reach their harmonic resolution, has here become the *pictorial content*.[8]

By such criteria, it makes little difference whether the 'sitter' for the portrait is Jerusalem or Linz (fig. 5, 6). The urban experience is the same everywhere. Nevertheless,

Fig. 10 *Vienna, State Opera*, 1956; oil on canvas, 82 x 115 cm.
Museum Moderner Kunst, Vienna

there were a handful of cities that provided Kokoschka with an exceptional stimulus. Apart from Dresden, the river views of which have already been mentioned, the cities that moved him to paint them repeatedly were London, Prague, Venice (see plates 53, 82), Amsterdam (see plate 52), Hamburg and, to a lesser extent, Vienna. His encounter with London, where he lived during the Second World War, extended over many years (see plates 86, 87); by contrast, his intensive concern with Prague (see plates 63-5, 68) was limited to his stay there between 1934 and 1938, after he had turned his back on the Austrian corporatist state and before the Nazi seizure of power forced him to flee to England.

Kokoschka's relationship with Vienna was an ambivalent one, and this finds expression in his work. In his six paintings of Vienna the city itself (with one exception, fig. 10) plays a subordinate role. He chooses landscape motifs in the Liebhartstal area, on the western outskirts, where Kokoschka lived with his family in the early 1930s (see fig. 7). The end of his first, 'voluntary' nomadic period was soon followed by an odyssey imposed by political circumstance.

After his wartime allegories of contemporary events Kokoschka turned back to the townscape as a central theme of his late work; like the portrait, this was a genre that stayed with him all his life. Alongside a number of works in which he reverts to his own established pictorial formulas, there is one small group of paintings that seems to contradict the principles enunciated above. In them the high viewpoint is maintained, but the picture is dominated by a single motif, shown in all its uniqueness: the Forum Romanum (fig. 8) or the Colosseum in Rome, the cathedral in Florence (fig. 9) or the State Opera in Vienna (fig. 10). Given a certain familiarity with Kokoschka's intentions, one soon realizes that these are no superficial depictions of tourist sights; they are evocations of the spiritual power of civilization, which endures through the centuries in the form of its monuments. A line can be traced from the remains of antiquity, still massive in their ruin, by way of the looming bulk of a Christian cathedral, to a latter-day temple of the arts that has survived the effects of war. *Vienna, State Opera*, a bastion in oblique perspective, recalls the ark in Paolo Uccello's *Deluge* fresco in Santa Maria Novella in Florence.

This group of works forms a logical link between the view of the world seen in Kokoschka's townscapes and the world-view expressed in the mythological themes of his late work. Like the human figures, the cities embody the creative act as a defiant riposte to defeat and decline. The 'assertion of life *in spite of everything*' is the message that Kokoschka reads in the eye of the vanquished Darius: 'I will not bow down! I cannot perish!'[9]

Notes

1 Quoted in Katharina Schulz, 'Chronology', in *Oskar Kokoschka 1886-1980*, exhibition catalogue, London, Tate Gallery, 1986, p. 348.

2 Quoted in *Oskar Kokoschka: Städteporträts*, exhibition catalogue, Vienna, Österreichisches Museum für angewandte Kunst, 1986, p. 8.

3 Ibid., p. 24.

4 See *Kokoschka: Städteporträts*, in which Kokoschka's paintings are juxtaposed with photographs taken from the same vantage-point. In many cases several shots were necessary in order to reproduce the visual angle of the painting.

5 Oskar Kokoschka, 'Das Auge des Darius: Altdorfers "Alexander-schacht"' (1956), in idem, *Das schriftliche Werk*, vol. 3, *Aufsätze, Vorträge, Essays zur Kunst*, Hamburg, 1975, pp. 85-92.

6 Ibid., p. 87.

7 Otto Pächt, *Rembrandt*, ed. Edwin Lachnit, Munich, 1991, p. 210.

8 Kokoschka, 'Das Auge des Darius', p. 88 f.

9 Ibid, p. 92.

Edwin Lachnit

The Power of Images

Political Involvement, 1931-1953

Painting as a Weapon

The dress rehearsal for the Second World War, mounted by the German Condor Legion 'high above the Spanish earth' in April 1937, left behind not only death and devastation in the Basque territory but a deep mark on the history of art. Spontaneously, Pablo Picasso turned the bombing of the city of Guernica into the theme of a monumental mural for the Spanish Pavilion at the World's Fair in Paris: or, rather, he gave that painting a title that related it to a contemporary event. For, as far as its content goes, *Guernica* is 'not a painting about modern war' but a generalized manifesto against brutality and rape, 'a painting about how Picasso *imagines* suffering'.[1]

Although a number of individual elements can be construed as allegorical allusions to the Spanish people,[2] *Guernica* is a statement that would be perfectly comprehensible without the immediate occasion that gave rise to it and without knowledge of its title. With all its potential for generalization, this entirely personal artistic reaction has in fact become 'a myth in the art history of this century' and 'laid the foundation of an artistic language of international anti-Fascism'.[3]

A generalized effect of this kind is in keeping with Picasso's own conviction of the artist's political function, which led him in 1944 to join the French Communist Party: 'What is an artist, as you see it? A fool who has nothing but eyes if he is a painter, or ears if he is a musician...? On the contrary, he is also a political being, always receptive to emotional or burning issues, or to happy events, to which he responds in every way....No, painting is not there to decorate apartments. It is a weapon for attack and defence against the enemy'.[4] With this ambitious statement, art declared its independence from the primacy of seen impressions and became a direct political instrument.

The same events that led Picasso to proclaim to the world his personal commitment prompted Kokoschka to work on a local level, with the traditional tools of political agitation. In Prague, where he had been living since 1934, he stuck up posters with the message (in Czech) *Help the Basque Children!* (fig. 1). This clear commitment was matched by an equally sober narrative image: a mother with two children, fleeing from the destruction visited upon them by a bomber that looms like an angel of death. The bomber, which appears in cropped form in the upper left-hand corner of the image, casts the shadow of its wings on the Prague skyline in the background and thus links the remote Spanish theatre of war with the (then still free) city of Central Europe.

In this way Kokoschka emphasizes the more than local significance of the use of terror against the Spanish civilian population; his primary intention, of course, is to underscore the intended appeal to the good nature of the citizens of Prague, but he clearly also means to give voice to the impending threat to the entire continent. This deliberately political act caused considerably less of a stir than did Picasso's Paris exhibit: fearful of a diplomatic incident, the Czech state police removed the posters from the walls after a few days.

Two other drawings by Kokoschka take up a similarly uncompromising political line: the portraits of the poet Federico García Lorca, murdered by the Falangists in 1936 (fig. 3), and of the legendary Communist politician Dolores Gómez Ibárruri (*La Pasionaria*; fig. 2). 'The murdered poet of

Fig. 1 *Help the Basque Children!*, 1937; colour lithograph, 103 x 74 cm

Fig. 2   *Dolores Gómez Ibárruri (La Pasionaria)*, 1937; pen and ink on paper. Dimensions and whereabouts unknown

the Spanish people' (to quote the inscription) rises up with fist clenched and with a look in which mute pain and impotent anger combine with the 'proletarian' resolve to resist the atrocities that are going on around him. This work, too, was meant as an explicit act of solidarity. Kokoschka added a further inscription: 'All reproduction rights assigned to Spanish organizations that defend the rights of the Spanish people against Fascist powers.—OK'. By comparison with this statement, a tribute to Lorca such as that paid by Renato Guttuso in his *Execution in the Countryside* of 1939,[5] with its typological precedents in the work of Goya and Manet, remains less explicit—for all its ostentatious welter of blood-red paint—and less intense in expression.

La Pasionaria combines the combative attitude of the Lorca portrait with the Prague poster's emphasis on the plight of children. Her clenched fist is balanced by a child held in the crook of her other arm, which turns the political thrust of the anti-Fascist fighter back upon the archetypal protective gesture of motherhood.

It is worth remembering the fundamental importance, in Kokoschka's whole world-view, of Johann Jakob Bachofen's work on matriarchy, *Mutterrecht* (Mother Right), and also of the teaching of the Moravian humanist Jan Amos Comenius. In the doom-laden atmosphere of the 1930s Kokoschka's educational ideals, based on Comenius, grew into a positive vision of the future and turned his painting of a children's home run by the Social Democratic city administration of Vienna, *Vienna, View from the Wilhelminenberg* (fig. 7, p. 33), into 'my first picture with a political mean-

ing'.[6] In his portrait of the Czech president, Tomáš G. Masaryk, painted in Prague on the eve of the Second World War (fig. 27, p. 222), those convictions hardened into a political manifesto.

Politics: A Problem of Form

Where he had once appealed on behalf of the victims of the Spanish Civil War, in 1938 and thereafter Kokoschka found himself coming to terms with his own experiences as an exile in England: 'During this period I painted a series of "political" pictures, not out of any political commitment, but with the intention of opening others' eyes to the way I saw the war'.[7]

In these works the element of political agitation in the drawings intended for reproduction gave way to the subjective act of perception—which, however, 'also included the depth of understanding implied in the term *Weltanschauung* (world-view); in other words not only receptiveness to a wide range of experience, but also an ability to transmute concrete, visible reality into pictorial parables and symbols'.[8]

Fig. 3   *Federico García Lorca*, 1936, pen and ink on paper, 28.5 x 18 cm. Národni Galerie v Praze, Prague

In a process that was diametrically opposed to Picasso's intentions, political reality was thus transformed into the problem of form in art. And that was how the message was received: 'People regarded his pictures as pictures, not as exhortations. In reality they are both, the one inseparable from the other'.[9] In its relation to current historical events Kokoschka's allegorical language is far less abstract than Picasso's, but it cannot be understood without a detailed knowledge of those events. Closely tied as it is to its historical and autobiographical context, this symbolism has brought a wild proliferation of exegesis in its train—notably because the artist himself was sparing with his explanations.[10]

One case in point is the painting *The Crab* (plate 79). The oddly shaped *objet trouvé* caught Kokoschka's eye on a walk along the beach; he took it home and recorded it in a watercolour study (1940, private collection). It became an allegory of menace only later, when he added a tiny figure swimming—or rather drowning—in the sea. It is this figure, to be identified as Kokoschka himself and founded on his own experience, that adds the political dimension. He represents Czechoslovakia; the crab (that is, the British prime minister, Neville Chamberlain) 'would only have to put out one claw to save him from drowning, but remains aloof'.[11]

Quite unequivocally, *The Red Egg* (plate 80) denounces the annihilation of Czechoslovakia in the autumn of 1938 by the Munich Agreement, in which Chamberlain and the French premier, Edouard Daladier (both represented here by symbolic animals) agreed with Hitler and Mussolini (shown as portrait likenesses) that the Sudetenland should be ceded to Germany; whereupon the Führer gave secret orders for 'the elimination of the Czech remnant'. In the background, as a prophetic reminder of the consequences suggested in the Basque poster, Prague burns.

The beacon that blazes in the background of *Anschluss— Alice in Wonderland* (plate 77) is similarly prophetic. The artist's only concrete reference here to contemporary events is to the *Anschluss* of March 1938: the annexation of Austria by Hitler's Germany. The inescapable consequences are indicated by a blazing building that stands (as the inscription on its classical pediment reveals) for the city of Vienna. Whether or not the building can be defined in topographical terms—perhaps as the Austrian parliament on the Ringstrasse—is less important here than Kokoschka's vision of Vienna as 'the frontier town of the ancient Roman Empire', whose historical task it was 'to transform knowledge, that Hellenic intellectual heritage, into a European inheritance and to convey it to an undivided humanity'.[12]

The brutal thwarting of that mission by the Nazi dictatorship is symbolized in Kokoschka's picture, painted in 1942, by the burning of a classical architectural motif. This was long before Vienna, in the last days of the war, was indeed reduced to rubble and ashes.

The alternative title, *Alice in Wonderland*, is harder to understand—although it must be remembered that the painting was intended for a British public, since at the time Kokoschka obviously had no access to a German (or *ostmär-*

Fig. 4 *What We Are Fighting For*, 1943; oil on canvas, 116.5 x 152 cm. Kunsthaus, Zurich

kisch, the Nazi word for Austrian) audience. Carroll's trustful heroine passes through a succession of metamorphoses into a realm of caprice and arbitrary rules, where people are put to silence, where 'nonsense takes on the mantle of logic, and the tyranny of rules assumes the semblance of legitimacy'.[13] Her grotesque adventures must have seemed entirely appropriate to Kokoschka as a way of presenting the fall of Austria to an English-speaking audience.

He was firmly convinced that Austria had been handed over to an expansionist Greater Germany as part of the Anglo-French policy of appeasement, an innocent 'pawn sacrifice' to Hitler.[14] Accordingly, the three helmeted 'air-raid warden' figures, one of them in morning dress, represent the accommodation between England, France and the Third Reich, but also the interlocking interests of Capital, the Military and the Church. With the familiar gestures of the three monkeys they stand aloof from the plight of poor Alice, who languishes behind barbed wire in the joint guise of 'German Womanhood' and a Red Cross volunteer. This know-nothing trio would not be out of place among the weird creatures whom Alice meets in the course of her adventures, nor would the mother and her gas-masked child in the lower left-hand corner.[15]

The diagonal that starts at that point, along which the heads of all the characters are aligned, ends at top right in a sinister void. The headless bodies of the Madonna and Child—their upright position suggests a desecrated altar, but blood flows from her severed neck—might also be an echo of Carroll's tale;[16] in any case, they represent the antithesis of the Nazi image of womanhood presented to us by the blond-plaited nude. The beheading of the Mother of God destroys the cult of the Great Mother, from which Kokoschka derives the humanistic essence of the Baroque civilization of Austria.[17]

Taken together, the two mother-and-child groups in the painting act, so to speak, as 'quotation marks', between which the abuse of sexual integrity (that is, national sovereignty) takes place. A second religious source, alongside the Madonna theme, is the story of Susanna and the Elders, but whereas the two voyeurs in the Apocryphal Old Testament tale gratify their lust by watching the chaste Susanna at her bath, here self-interest is so all-consuming that the naked woman is ignored.

In *What We Are Fighting For* (fig. 4) the crucifixion of the matriarchal order of society is complete. In the course of the sequence the mother figure has fled from the bombing of a Basque city, has frozen into an icon of defiance in the person of *La Pasionaria* and has tried to protect her child with its hideous gas mask, only to be butchered in effigy in the aftermath of the *Anschluss*; now she lies dying in abject misery on the ground. Her fruitless maternal care is echoed by her child, who nurses a rat. The postures of the two figures, isolated on an ochre ground and linked only outwardly, contain formal reminiscences of *The Tempest* (plate 25). In that very different context the drapes that swathe the reclining couple have been likened to a shroud.[18]

In the vast gulf that separates misery from those who cause it, the mechanisms of war policy grind on implacably. A bishop doles out small change to the Red Cross with his left hand, and with his right blesses the troops who march off to war; a little further on they march into captivity with hands raised. Companionably, the financiers of rearmament—Montague Norman, Governor of the Bank of England, and the president of the German Reichsbank, Hjalmar Schacht—observe the scene from a distance, accompanied by a marshal of France. Mahatma Gandhi is the coolie who drags the imperialist rickshaw. At the far left the armaments industry plies its world-wide trade in the form of 'a globe-like monster'. At the top it pulls out 'a blue rabbit signifying peace, as an emblem of hope for the future'; below, it devours human bones and churns out munitions. Opposite, in the right foreground, a bust of Voltaire evokes that writer's satirical novel *Candide*, in which he confronts 'the best of all possible worlds' in all its vileness.[19]

This painting was Kokoschka's contribution to the exhibition 'For Liberty', mounted by the Artists' International Association in London in 1943. A cynical and melancholy answer to the question 'What Are We to Fight For?', it marked his withdrawal from politics and social criticism: 'Let me say once more that I did not paint these pictures because I felt a political involvement of any specific kind. I was staying in England only in order to see war this time from the other side of the barricades.... Unlike George Grosz, who painted his whores and his fat, lustful bourgeois in Berlin in time of peace, and in a spirit of criticism and hatred, I raised my voice in London in wartime because the time and the circumstances made it imperative to become human once again.'[20]

Against Inhumanity, not For an Ideology

Kokoschka's renunciation of political commitment was the result of a long prehistory, and it is no accident that Grosz's name is mentioned in the passage just quoted. During the troubles in the Weimar Republic, on 15 March 1920 a painting by Rubens in the Zwinger in Dresden was damaged by a stray bullet. Kokoschka, then a professor at the Dresden academy, issued the following appeal: 'I request all those who intend to use firearms in order to promote their political beliefs, whether of the radical left, the radical right or the radical centre, to be kind enough to hold their military exercises elsewhere than in front of the art gallery in the Zwinger: for instance, on the shooting-ranges on the heath, where human civilization is in no danger.'[21]

From the ranks of the revolutionary artists, John Heartfield and George Grosz countered at once with an onslaught on the cultural values of the bourgeoisie and directed their own 'urgent request to all those who are not yet so cretinized as to applaud this Art Thug's snobbish utterance to speak out vigorously against it'.[22] This did not prevent Heartfield, in exile in Prague in 1937, from joining an 'Oskar Kokoschka-Bund' which, under a cultural cover, worked as a Communist-dominated political underground movement and to which the eponymous artist did not himself belong.[23] It can safely be assumed, however, that Kokoschka did declare his solidarity in principle with the efforts of a united anti-Fascist front.

Retreating from the advance of Nazism, the émigré scene moved to London, and there Kokoschka took on the presidency of the Free German League of Culture (Freier Deutscher Kulturbund), one of whose activists was, again, Heartfield. There can be no doubt that at this stage Kokoschka did take to heart some party-political ideas. Among these was the critique of capitalism that emerges from such a title as *Private Property* of 1939/40,[24] as well as the demand, articulated in *Marianne—Maquis* of 1942,[25] that after the entry of the Soviets into the war a Second Front should be set up with the aid of the French Resistance.

As a whole, however, Kokoschka's art, in its unvarnished directness, strikes an existential rather than a political note. It pillories not so much a specific criminal regime as a general inhumanity that thrives in the space between the commission of a crime and its condonation. Its central message is not ideological propaganda but the need to bring to people's consciousness that mother and child are archetypes of existence, independent of any 'political' relevance.

The end of the Nazi menace did not change the criteria that Kokoschka had applied ever since his drawings for Spain. In the winter of 1945 the poster *Christ Helps the Starving Children* (fig. 28, p. 223) was posted in the London Underground stations as an appeal for donations to feed hungry children all over Europe. In the autumn of 1956, with *The Madonna in a Street Battle*,[26] he appealed for support for the victims of the rape of Hungary.

What did change at the end of the Second World War was that Kokoschka's allegories dispensed with their contemporary costume. *The Unleashing of Atomic Energy* of 1946/7[27] shows a circus clown opening the wild beasts' cage and, like the Sorcerer's Apprentice in Goethe's poem, unleashing forces beyond his control. There is also an unmistakable allusion to the apocalypse of Hiroshima: the escaping beast

Fig. 5 *Hades and Persephone* and *Prometheus*, 1950 (left and right panels of *The Prometheus Saga*);
oil on canvas, each 230 x 230 cm. Courtauld Institute Galleries, London

is about to pounce on a mother-Madonna with Asian features, who forms a Raphaelesque group with her child.

A few years later Kokoschka's appeal to hubristic modern man to 'know thyself' assumed the garb of Greek mythology, interwoven with the pictorial traditions of the Christian West. The triptych *The Prometheus Saga* (see fig. 5) and its historical derivation from Franz Anton Maulbertsch's late Baroque ceiling painting in the Piaristenkirche in Vienna have already formed the subject of an exhaustive analysis.[28] The central panel, with its apocalyptic vision, is flanked on the right by the punishment of Prometheus for his presumption and on the left by the realm of nature, in which Demeter, Persephone and Medusa 'are caught up in the cycle of life, death, and rebirth'.

Once again, this confrontation between the male power principle and the female life principle has an almost exactly contemporary analogy in the work of Picasso. In *Massacre in Korea* of 1951[29] Picasso's group of women and children standing before a firing squad has its art historical precedents in the execution scenes of Goya and Manet. Yet, like Guttuso before him, Picasso fails to recapture his predecessors' emotional intensity. The soldiers' archaic, utopian dress removes the scene into the remote and unreal world of modern fantasy films and neutralizes the contemporary political relevance that the title (an afterthought) was intended to achieve. Similarly, Picasso's pair of frieze-like paintings *War* and *Peace* of 1952[30] achieve mythological timelessness at the expense of topical impact. 'Equally unsuccessful was the attempt to construct a new mythological being, a *Face of Peace*, from the fusion of a woman's head and a dove of peace, as seen in a lithograph of 1951. And so Picasso never succeeded in creating a second *Guernica*.'[31]

By contrast, the antique concerns of Kokoschka's late work fit seamlessly into the overall context of his artistic world-view. This is not the sort of a late work in which an urgent youthful commitment has frozen into a set of remote stereotypes; it is an advanced stage in a continuing process of visualization. *The Prometheus Saga* stands at the end of an unbroken evolution that can be traced back through the 'political' paintings to the Dresden period, if not earlier: 'From the standpoint of life in society I have come to the conclusion, as an active participant in the First World War and a passive participant in the Second World War, that it remains the task of the visual artist to give form to the experience of seeing and, in a wider sense, to existence itself'.[32]

All his life, from his romantic zeal to capture in words 'The Awareness of Visions'[33] to his practical work as an educator at the School of Seeing in Salzburg, Kokoschka obeyed his vocation as a seer. On the left-hand panel of *The Prometheus Saga* that vocation—which he equates in importance with the task of giving 'form to existence'—gives the artist the strength of the Mothers to dispel the 'dissolution, destruction, typification and atomization of personal life'[34] and to arise from the throes of death, calling out his appeal to us; meanwhile Prometheus, in the helpless weakness of his exaggerated notion of self, lets slip the stolen firebrand that threatens to plunge the whole world in flames.

Leitmotiv: Strength and Weakness

The confrontation between strength and weakness runs through Kokoschka's painting from beginning to end. In 1920 he gave the title *Strength and Weakness* to the painting that later became known as *The Power of Music* (plate 42).

Fig. 6 *The Battle*, 1954 (central panel of *Thermopylae*); oil on canvas, 225 x 300 cm.
University of Hamburg

Three decades before *The Prometheus Saga* this key work combines all the elements that appear severally in the 'Humanity' paintings of the post-war period. A female figure with a trumpet irresistibly imparts life to a half-enfeebled, half-reluctant youth, who sets out to carry the spiritual message beyond the confines of the picture. Music, whose invigorating properties are made visible in the colour, is female, as is art in general. 'To him [Kokoschka] there are no arts, but only one Art, which finds expression in such different media as sound, colour and sculptural form.'[35] The power of music is the power of painting is the power of the artist.

It is a power that Kokoschka exercises for no less a purpose than to stabilize the shaken foundations of civilization itself. In 1954 he painted *Thermopylae* (see fig. 6) for a lecture room in the Philosophy Tower of Hamburg University: another large triptych on a subject taken from classical antiquity. Although the subject is the devoted self-sacrifice of the Greek army under Leonidas in the face of an overwhelmingly superior Persian force, and although the right-hand panel looks forward to the saving of Greece by Themistocles' naval victory at Salamis, this is neither a history painting nor a battle piece. True, in its conception Kokoschka 'concentrates primarily on the Cold War of the 1950s' and on 'the ideology of the Adenauer era',[36] but—as with the wartime allegories—beneath the political surface there lie far deeper layers of meaning. It is on this deeper level that classical antiquity is represented in this work by an event that marked a decisive test of the endurance of Western culture, which is

no more limited chronologically than Europe is limited geographically. Thanks to the special nature of Greek art—the meaning of

which was not merely aesthetic but ethical, coinciding with that of the State and of the wider comity of human beings—what we find in the depiction of victors and vanquished alike is ourselves.... Herodotus' history of the Persian Wars was not a piece of war reporting. These battles were not fought for the cause of Hellenic national unity, nor for the preservation of economic interests, nor for ideologies. Unlike the wars of modern times, which owe their origins and their continuation to a lack of foresight, the fifty-year war against the Persians was fought, as Herodotus shows us, over the distinction between the human being and the barbarian.[37]

In the triptych as executed the painter accentuated his appeal to his contemporaries even more strongly. The figure of Herodotus,[38] who had appeared in one of the sketches for the work, was to form the subject of a painting in its own right.[39] Herodotus was replaced at the left-hand side of the central panel by Megistias: the historian gave way to the seer who predicted the defeat of the Greek army. The central axis of the action is occupied by the 'Delayer', caught in a pose of doubt and hesitation, conscious of the danger but still lacking the resolve to take a decisive hand in the action. Once more, the strength of insight confronts the weakness of action.

Between these two poles lies the power of images: power as a defensive weapon, as in Picasso's case, or as an instructive parable, as in Kokoschka's. In social terms the work of art can seem to inspire or to conspire, and in either case it generates unease. 'To this day... the fear of images is as powerful as the longing to have them.'[40] In Spain the celebrations and exhibitions that greeted Picasso's ninetieth birthday in 1971 led to 'arrests of, and also assaults on, Picasso sympathizers, and the destruction of his works by right-wing extremists'.[41] The foundation of a documentary archive in Kokoschka's birthplace at Pöchlarn in 1973 actually brought out into the open a League Against Degenerate Art.[42]

Even so, the artist's intellectual authority has no impact on practical politics. Picasso's *Guernica* did nothing to avert My Lai, nor did Kokoschka's Dresden protest prevent the devastation of the National Gallery in Bucharest in December 1989.

Here, none the less, lies the source of the endlessly renewed social challenge of artistic creation (*die bildende Kunst*, which for Kokoschka was both the art that shapes objects and the art that shapes people). Through art we counter the brute force of barbarism with humanity, as manifest in the power of form; through art, instead of abdicating in the face of the intractable, we illuminate it by representing it.

Notes

1 John Berger, *The Success and Failure of Picasso*, Harmondsworth, 1965, pp. 166, 168.
2 See Wilfried Wiegand, *Pablo Picasso in Selbstzeugnissen und Bilddokumenten*, Reinbek, 1973, p. 111, n. 167.
3 Wiegand, *Picasso*, p. 113.
4 Quoted in Wiegand, *Picasso*, p. 122. A comprehensive study of Picasso's politics is provided by Ludwig Ullmann, 'Der Krieg im Werk Picassos: Reaktionen auf Krieg und Verfolgung', Ph.D. diss., Osnabrück, 1986.
5 Renato Guttuso, *Fucilazione in Campagna*; oil on canvas, 100 x 75 cm; Galleria Nazionale d'Arte Moderna, Rome.
6 Edith Hoffmann, *Kokoschka: Life and Work*, London, 1947, p. 197.
7 Oskar Kokoschka, *My Life*, trans. David Britt, London and New York, 1974, p. 164.
8 Werner Hofmann, 'The Knight Errant', in *Oskar Kokoschka 1886-1980*, exhibition catalogue, London, Tate Gallery, 1986, p. 13.
9 Ibid., p. 18.
10 Kokoschka, *My Life*, p. 164f. See also Robert Radford, 'Kokoschka's Political Allegories', *Art Monthly* (June 1986), pp. 3-6.
11 Kokoschka, quoted in *Oskar Kokoschka 1886-1980*, exhibition catalogue, London, Tate Gallery, 1986, p. 320, cat. 87; the watercolour study is cat. 204.
12 Oskar Kokoschka, 'Die Prometheus Saga, 1952', in idem, *Das schriftliche Werk*, vol. 3, *Aufsätze, Vorträge, Essays zur Kunst*, Hamburg, 1975, p. 318f. There is an analogy in the architectural historian's view that the 'element of classical antiquity' that decisively influenced the design of Theophil Hansen's parliament building of 1869-83 was 'rooted in the cultural atmosphere of Vienna': Renate Wagner-Rieger, 'Der Architekt Theophil Hansen', *Anzeiger der österreichischen Akademie der Wissenschaften, Phil.-hist. Klasse* 114, no. 8 (1977), p. 260.
13 Christian Enzensberger, 'Der Aufruhr der Regeln', afterword to Lewis Carroll, *Alice im Wunderland*, Frankfurt am Main, 1973, pp. 129-38.
14 Significantly, in the sequel to *Alice in Wonderland*, *Through the Looking-Glass*, Alice is compelled to conform to the rules of chess.
15 In the former case there are the characters in 'A Mad Tea-Party'; in the latter there is the Duchess, whose baby changes into a pig (*Alice in Wonderland*, chapters 6, 7).
16 Under the despotic rule of the Queen of Hearts, as Alice observes, 'They're dreadfully fond of beheading people here; the great wonder is, that there's anyone left alive!' (ibid., chapter 8.)
17 See Hofmann, 'The Knight Errant', and Almut Krapf-Weiler, 'Zur Bedeutung des österreichischen Barock für Oskar Kokoschka', *Wiener Jahrbuch für Kunstgeschichte* 40 (1987), pp. 195-208.
18 Hofmann, 'The Knight Errant', p. 14. On the significance of yellow as a colour of death, see Kokoschka, *My Life*, p. 165.
19 Kokoschka, *My Life*, p. 165.
20 Ibid.
21 Oskar Kokoschka, 'An die Einwohnerschaft Dresdens' (1920), in idem, *Das schriftliche Werk*, vol. 4, *Politische Äusserungen*, Hamburg, 1976, p. 31; this passage trans. in Kokoschka, *My Life*, p. 111.
22 John Heartfield and George Grosz, 'Der Kunstlump', *Der Gegner* 1, nos. 10-12 (1919), p. 53, repr. Berlin, 1979.
23 See Werner Haftmann, *Verfemte Kunst: Bildende Künstler der inneren und äusseren Emigration in der Zeit des Nationalsozialismus*, Cologne, 1986, p. 75f.
24 Oil on canvas, 63 x 76 cm; inscribed 'OK' l.r. and 'PRIVATE PROPERTY by OK 1939' on back of canvas; private collection.
25 Oil on canvas, 63.5 x 76 cm; inscribed 'OK' l.l., 'Maquis by O.K./ 1942' across back of canvas and 'Second Front' on stretcher; private collection.
26 *Madonna im Strassenkampf*; colour lithograph, 50.5 x 42.7 cm; inscribed 'L'Enfant de Bethleem, 1956' l.c. and c.r.
27 *Entfesselung der Atomenergie*; oil on canvas, 61 x 91 cm; inscribed 'OK' l.r.; Bezalel Museum, Jerusalem.
28 Werner Hofmann, 'Der irrende Ritter', in *Oskar Kokoschka: Symposion*, ed. Erika Patka, Salzburg and Vienna, 1986, pp. 265-78; Krapf-Weiler, 'Bedeutung'; also Kokoschka, 'Die Prometheus Saga'.
29 Oil on plywood, 110 x 210 cm; Musée Picasso, Paris.
30 Oil on fibreboard, each 470 x 1020 cm; Temple de la Paix, Vallauris.
31 Wiegand, *Picasso*, p. 129.
32 Kokoschka, 'Die Prometheus Saga', p. 317.
33 Idem, *Aufsätze*, pp. 9-33.
34 Idem, 'Die Prometheus Saga', p. 317. Any psychoanalytical explanation of Kokoschka's belief that the visionary faculties belong to the maternal sphere must give due weight to the fact that both his mother and his grandmother were said to possess 'the gift of second sight'; see Kokoschka, *My Life*, p. 13f.
35 Krapf-Weiler, 'Bedeutung', p. 196.
36 Hofmann, 'The Knight Errant', p. 14.
37 Oskar Kokoschka, 'Zu meinem Triptychon [*Thermopylae*]' (1955), in idem, *Aufsätze*, p. 323f.
38 Carl Georg Heise, *Oskar Kokoschka: Thermopylae 1954*, Stuttgart, 1961, fig. 9.
39 *Herodot*, 1964; oil on canvas, 18 x 20 cm.; inscribed on back of canvas 'O.K. 25.12.1963. So treibt's die Menschheit/sagt Herodot/ich auch' (That's how humankind carries on, says Herodotus—me too); Österreichische Galerie, Vienna.
40 Werner Hofmann, 'Produktive Konflikte', in *Kunsthistoriker in eigener Sache: Zehn autobiographische Skizzen*, ed. Martina Sitt, Berlin, 1990, p. 125.
41 Wiegand, *Picasso*, p. 123.
42 'Liga gegen entartete Kunst', leaflet dated 14 July 1973; Oskar Kokoschka-Dokumentation, Pöchlarn.

Johann Winkler

The Fires of Colour

On the Late Work, 1953-1973

For Oskar Kokoschka art and life were an indivisible unity: 'For this towering giant, profoundly moved as he was by the irretrievable uniqueness of every visual experience, every encounter with the visible world was a new adventure; for what is seen and the person who sees are both transformed with every passing instant.'[1] Progressively, as he learned more of the extent and depth of external and internal reality in humankind and in the world, this sensed and learned actuality took shape in his art. The fleeting and fortuitous vision could be made to last only through his alertness and openness to the true, comprehended, consciously grasped 'vital experience' in life: 'Only our vital experience truly belongs to us! Whatever it may have been like: what we take into our inner life is stored there!'[2]

In the same text Kokoschka went on to say, with reference to six self-portraits executed between 1912 and 1917: 'Even I did not deliberately set out to paint these seven pictures of myself, at different times, like stones strung together; and I am glad, today, to find in them something, like a scarlet thread, that fits into my history'.[3]

Step by step, Kokoschka's subjective view of the world expanded into a unity that welded together 'the sensory with the conceptual'.[4] Increasingly, the outer eye, directed towards the world of being, came to coincide with the vision that rests on the inner essence of people and things. The dialectic of this process was observed long ago, but it was misinterpreted as a conflict between mutually exclusive positions, instead of being understood as a unified, logical, transformative evolution. In Kokoschka the inner and outer worlds combine as naturally as do the old and the new. Progress and the longing to be a fruitful continuer of the Old Master tradition are simply two sides of a single phenomenon. The radical quality of the early portraits emerged in 1909 from the 'courage to resist the pressure of old habits of seeing',[5] and did so with the same compelling force with which his later works resisted the 'still seductive pressure of new fashions'[6] by reasserting traditional positions.

Hans Tietze was right when, in 1930, he surveyed the reputation of the then 44-year-old Kokoschka and concluded: 'This man, who once burst in upon the safe hereditaments of tradition, almost as an infant prodigy, is now cast aside as one of the older generation; yesterday's revolutionary now finds himself confronted with today's radicals'.[7] Yet Tietze went on to say that it is the very nature of exceptional gifts 'to realize the unique quality of every successive stage in life with particular intensity', and ventured a glimpse of the future: 'It may yet turn out to be Kokoschka's destiny to find that his tumultuous youth, which swept us off our feet, is matched in his old age by works in which a far-away gaze seems to encompass visions of the beyond'.[8]

In Kokoschka's work acquired knowledge and mental horizons had expanded concentrically. In portraiture he had opened up new dimensions and crossed into areas that had previously been taboo. The stages of his subsequent evolution had been marked by love and its bitter end; near-death and loss of bearings amid the horrors of war; a renewed faith in the omnipotence of art, painfully extracted in Dresden from the blaze of hitherto unheard-of colour chords; and the bold stride forward into the light-filled, 'cosmic' spaces of the cities and landscapes of Europe and North Africa.

Then, in response to the political upheavals and catastrophes of the 1930s and 1940s, and as a reaction to being outlawed and forced into exile by the Nazis, he developed a growing concern with contemporary history—and, after the Second World War, also with the philosophy of civilization—that took the form of an endeavor to achieve 'social impact':

The terse formulations of the early Expressionist paintings and writings—in which critics choose to see the true Kokoschka—have been extended into vast, symbolic structures of action.... This late

Fig. 1 Rembrandt, *Self-Portrait at the Age of Sixty-Three*, 1669; oil on canvas, 86 x 70.5 cm. National Gallery, London

work is not an appendix; it is a rich fulfilment and diversification of the world outlined in the early dramas, and it also deepens and elevates that world on to a universal scale of meaning. The *Prometheus* ceiling . . . and the *Thermopylae* triptych in Hamburg are among the most significant images of their time; in them individual testimony is elevated into a message to humanity at large.[9]

Freedom at the Price of Safety

In 1953 Kokoschka moved to a house at Villeneuve, near Montreux, with extensive views over Lake Geneva. This decision to let down roots at last, after nearly seventy years as a nomad, can surely be seen as his decisive break with the past, and thus defines the beginning of the late work as such.

It was no coincidence that the first painting he began at Villeneuve, the *Thermopylae* triptych (see fig. 6, p. 42), posed the question of man's responsibility to himself, to his fellow citizens, even to humanity. With its message that freedom belongs only to those who defy danger and even destruction to make use of it, this triptych exemplifies Kokoscha's own audacious resolve to pursue the 'scarlet thread' of his own life, even—or especially—in stern defiance of the demands of the Zeitgeist.

Like *The Prometheus Saga* (see fig. 5, p. 41), painted shortly before, this triptych was an 'act constituting order and

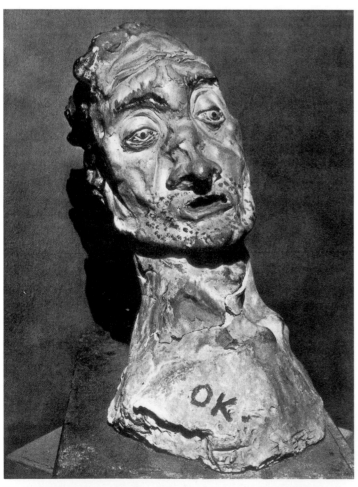

Fig. 2 *Self-Portrait as a Warrior*, 1908; clay, painted with tempera, height 36.5 cm. Museum of Fine Arts, Boston, Bequest of J. H. and E. A. Payne

meaning'[10] which seemed to offset the anti-traditional beginnings of the artist's own career by reverting, once and for all, to the very traditionalism that had once seemed so utterly outworn. What was really happening was a last, decisive expansion of the concentric circles of Kokoschka's work and life. Out of the seeming equilibrium of progression and regression, extraversion and introversion, there surged a blaze of new energy that restored to Kokoschka's late work all the radical spontaneity of his youth.

In these works colour takes on a decisive significance as the vehicle both of symbolic expression and of the now all-powerful light. Once more, the painter holds the balance between an outward and an inward gaze: outward, pursuing the image of the world of the senses in all its beauty; inward—and with the same intensity that had so alarmed the sitters who commissioned his early portraits—towards the self. As one writer has put it: 'Perhaps the uniqueness of Kokoschka's art consists in the tension between the impetuous gesture, which seeks to express the outward and inward vision with scant regard for any pleasantness of line, and the tireless quest for the light-filled image that he loved with such fiery passion'.[11]

In an interview Kokoschka himself told the journalist Ben Witter: 'To me painting is lighting a fire . . . . I transform myself—something transforms itself inside me . . . . Others grow old, but I can't grow old . . . . After the explosion of an atom bomb perhaps a glass, by me, will remain: a glass, as I have seen it and painted it; and I tell myself: for all you know, you as a document may be the only person who survives . . . . The world does not exist without me, and it has had a long time to wait for me'.[12]

Once more, the beginning and the end are united. The circle encompasses art and life as an indivisible whole, neither capable of existing without the other. The marvellous idea of comparing the process of painting—which is to say, that of art, and thus of life—to the lighting of a fire leads, by virtue of the associative richness of the metaphor, straight to the stylistic character and essence of Kokoschka's work, and of the late work in particular.

The life-preserving aspect of fire, its ability to keep danger and death at bay, is just as evident here as is its ability to cleanse and also to annihilate. At the same time, the red flame evokes the 'primeval colour', that of blood and passion, which stands symbolically for life itself, and which consequently always held special importance for Kokoschka.

The works of Kokoschka's last period include portraits, such as that of the English publisher Sir Stanley Unwin of 1959,[13] and townscapes, such as the view of London (plate 86) looking down the Thames from the airy perspective of the Shell-Mex building at a metropolitan scene pulsing with life and movement and culminating in the magnificent dome of St Paul's on the horizon against a bright, opening sky. They also include allegories, such as *Storm Tide in Hamburg* (plate 85) or the subtly allusive *The Frogs* (plate 93). In all these Kokoschka reverted to subjects and themes that had been common in his earlier work.[14] Forcefully and unequivocally, these paintings confirm the aged seer's unflagging eagerness to explore the mysteries that lie hidden behind appearances, the inner cohesion of the universe.

In contrast to these works there is a last, self-contained and very different group of paintings in which Kokoschka's life story rounds itself off and finds, as Hans Tietze prophesied, a visionary fulfilment.

Exorcism as Self-Assertion

'I'm painting again, I've got over the "end of my life"',[15] wrote the artist to Heinz Spielmann from Villeneuve on 2 November 1971 after recovering from a serious illness. The painting to which he was referring, and which he completed during the winter of 1971/2, is a late masterpiece of overwhelming force and richness of allusion. The 'self-possessed refusal to compromise' of this work, and of the others in this final group, brought Kokoschka's individualistic *ultima maniera* into line with the contemporary avant-garde. *Time, Gentlemen, Please* (plate 87), so called in sardonic reference to the traditional cry of the English pub landlord at closing time, is Kokoschka's last and most extreme 'audacity': it strikes up a dialogue with the inexorable harbinger of the artist's own death.

The fires of self-assertion blaze out against the demon who opens the door into the netherworld. Once and for all, paint-ing becomes 'what it was in its remote beginnings: the act of formal creation once more includes an apotropaic element, and the artefact can serve to exorcize demons'.[16]

The self-portrait here is a purely painterly creation; it evolves from the sweep of a single gesture. A powerful red suffuses the artist's figure as the motive force of his unstoppable forward thrust; it is flecked with autumnal shades of brown, the symbols of transience. The yellow that flickers in the background as a curse and a warning has also been absorbed into the body, lending bulk and protection but also reducing its materiality. At the same time, the yellow in the centre is the mark of the artist's death-sentence. The blue on the open door hints at the darkness of the approaching night, as do the dark tones and white highlights in the face of death's youthful messenger, who seems to be in danger of being overwhelmed by the sheer vitality of the wraith that he has come to claim. Yet at the end of this perennially unequal contest there can be only one victor.

What Kokoschka says of Rembrandt's last self-portraits (see fig. 1) applies to his own late work: 'How is it possible to look so steadily into the face of death—one's own face? . . . If an artist is able to look the truth straight in the eye in such a way as to understand transience and still give form to it, and still make the immortal transparent within the mortal form, then he has done more than any word can do'.[17]

Fig. 3 Study for *Pietà, c.* 1908; charcoal on paper, dimensions unknown. Private collection, Vienna

Fig. 4 *Woman Leading Man*, 1914 (study for *Bach Cantata*); chalk on paper, 48.3 x 31.5 cm. Private collection, Germany

Fig. 5 *The Painter II* (*The Artist and his Model II*), 1923/4; oil on canvas, 85.5 x 130.5 cm.
The Saint Louis Art Museum

Time, Gentlemen, Please is a painting whose deepest layers go far back into Kokoschka's earliest youth. This archetypal invocation conjures up memories of the painted terra-cotta *Self-Portrait as a Warrior* of 1908 (fig. 2), of the bleeding Man of Sorrows in the *Pietà* of 1909 (see fig. 3)[18] and of the unsparing self-exposure of the 1910 poster for *Der Sturm*.[19] The outcast nomad of *Bach Cantata* (see fig. 4) appears before our inward eye,[20] and in the figure of the ageless old man, its effect intensified by a dislocation of proportion, we recognize the artist who appears in *The Painter II* of 1923/24 (fig. 5) and the clownish individual, with Kokoschka's own features, who creeps up behind the woman in *The Slave Girl* with such forlorn lewdness (fig. 10, p. 25). Time is suspended in a continuity that means something more than mere continuation: in its end it finds new beginnings, retrieving phenomena from the utmost recesses of consciousness and abruptly restoring them to the faculty of 'vision'. As Martin Gregor-Dellin has put it: 'Growing old also means keeping one's promises; but there is also a new spontaneity, which is not the same as untrammelled subjectivity, but which is simply indifferent to all that is formulaic, simultaneously using it and disregarding it'.[21]

In this free and spontaneous interplay of memory and imagination the late, introverted Kokoschka finds such images as the delightfully restrained and poetic *Two Girls with Dove* (plate 88), the instructive anecdote of *The Sailor*'s Bride (plate 92) or the elegant, sparkling wit of *The Rejected Lover* (plate 89). A joyous light, dappled with the shadows of gentle melancholy, fills these painted *divertimenti*; these are chamber-music delights that eschew all grand symphonic effects without thereby sacrificing intensity. Their harmonies, assembled from the primaries red and blue in multi-ple refractions and subtlest nuances, are based on warm-toned chords in which—interposed, juxtaposed and superimposed—all the colors of the spectrum glimmer and vibrate in sympathy.

Echoes of Youth

For a number of the major graphic cycles of his late period Kokoschka chose subjects from world literature,[22] exploring his own mission through a dialogue with their timeless protagonists, King Lear (see fig. 6), Odysseus, Saul, David, Achilles and Pan; in the telling of their tangled lives, he unravelled the threads of his own destiny.

On one occasion the octogenarian Kokoschka was prompted to explore the ground of his being and of his creativity by seeing a youthful work of his own. *The Power of Music* (plate 42), which he had completed in Dresden in 1920, brought him back to the one great, dominant theme of his career: the idea of living for and through art.

Morning and Evening (plate 90) is the evocative title of the variant he painted in 1966, which reverses the original composition. The female trumpet-blower of *The Power of Music*, an 'archangel of the Annunciation',[23] whose overwhelming summons seemed to put its boy recipient to flight, is now replaced by a youth, who serenades an enigmatic, statuesque female figure. Time stands still. The chapleted musician looks like an ancient demigod. The woman stands aloof; the pomegranate that she holds like a sceptre in her right hand identifies her as the personification of divine beauty, while the tones of white that dominate her face and torso carry her away into a near-inaccessible sphere of chastity. The vigorous gesture of simultaneous rejection and acceptance that

Fig. 6 *King Lear*, 1963; lithograph, 37.9 x 26.1 cm (image)

Fig. 7 *The Power of Music* (*Morning and Evening*), 1966; lithograph, 46.1 x 57.8 cm (image)

greets the trumpet's summons in *The Power of Music* of 1920 has resolved itself, at least superficially, into an idyll. In *Morning and Evening* the dramatic movement has come to a halt, though it remains visible in the divergent poses of the figures in the lithograph that Kokoschka produced at the same time (fig. 7).[24]

However, thanks to the gestural expressiveness of the open brushwork, with its exclusive allegiance to the inner vision, the pictorial space is full of the vital fire of music, whose insinuating, masterful, alluring sound reaches to the very doors of heaven. The Anima figure listens raptly, still caught in a pose of disembodied stillness, but the pomegranate in her hand, which is a symbol of life and fertility, assures her suitor, so intent on his music, that she is receptive and will respond to his signal by awakening to earthly life.

Morning and Evening is a parable of creation. Music—which, by extension, also means painting—is interpreted as a divine mission; it binds the order of the world into the harmony of the universe. However much the two paintings may differ in the nature of their endeavour to make spiritual and psychic forces visible—the one physically compact and enclosed, but pointing far beyond its own space through the gesture of awakening; the other classically severe in composition, but open to the infinite through the texture of the paint—the message that they proclaim is a single confession of creative faith.

It comes as no surprise, therefore, to find that the words of one critic at the time of Kokoschka's first major retrospective, at the Galerie Arnold in Dresden in 1925, have retained their validity: 'This is painting that is conceived purely in terms of colour. And yet the colour harmonies are not there for the sake of play or decoration; they are there for their expressive value, their symbolic content. The current work and the earliest work—utterly different though they seem—have this in common: in both, what we see is not exclusively an aesthetic, sensuous phenomenon but a pointer, a bridge to a realm beyond the senses.'[25]

Kokoschka himself wrote of Edvard Munch: 'Expressionism is the shaping of vital experience, and is thus mediated, a message from the I to the Thou. As with love, this takes two. Expressionism does not live in an ivory tower; it addresses itself to a fellow human being, whom it awakens.'[26] He could have found no better words in which to express his own artistic impulse.

Peer Gynt: Departure and Return

On New Year's Day 1969 Kokoschka began work on his last self-portrait in the narrow sense of the term (plate 83). The foreground is dominated by his own figure, displaced off-centre to the right, dramatically viewed from below and cut off below the hands that cross on his chest. The tones of blue in his high-necked smock symbolize mind and maleness, also imagination and the Romantic yearning to discover the world through the spirit of poetry and to follow the inner thread of fate to a destiny that transcends the merely personal. The features, however, betray tension and uncertainty. The 'X-ray eye', now directed solely at the artist's own self, is divided once more between the right eye, opened wide to look inwards, and the left eye, sceptically perusing his outer appearance; and this is the true content of the painting. It bears witness to the fragmented nature of the artist's being; it acknowledges the duality of existence.

Fig. 8 *Peer Gynt*, 1973 (study for the painting of the same title, plate 86); pencil on paper, 42 x 30 cm. Private collection, Switzerland

He is confronted by the antithetical symbols of light and darkness: a woman and a devil. The middle ground between them is the focus of the tension that arrests the eye and finds its reflection in the mirror of the artist's face. The woman, who is the embodiment and promise of living warmth, is the closer of the two figures in space. One glance from her is enough, for the moment, to banish the devil to the right-hand edge of the painting. The background, in deceptively shimmering violet—a colour that is entirely absent, as a local hue, from Kokoschka's paintings—and with menacing traces of black, is indication enough that the trial of strength is not over. The demon will return, and ultimately it will not be as a tempter but as a harbinger of death.

Just once more, the life and fire of Kokoschka's art puts him to flight. In the waking dream of *Peer Gynt* (plate 94; see also fig. 8) the hero leaves his mother, Åse, and Solveig, the girl who loves him; as the wild geese fly south, he hastens towards the light with arms upraised:

> I'll be with you! I'll wash myself clean
> In a bath of scouring wind! I'll go up and plunge right in
> To that bright baptismal font![27]

At this last moment of setting forth, the face of the waiting Åse, which has the features of the aged Kokoschka, is an anticipation of the ultimate return. Once more, beginning and end flow into one:

> Forward or back, it's the same distance;
> Out or in, it's equally narrow.[28]

Returning home at last, Peer meets himself at his mother's deathbed and is transformed back into the eternal wanderer Oskar Kokoschka, who called the world his own and whose life's work it was to see and to make others see.

Notes

1 Ernst Gombrich, 'Gedenkworte für Oskar Kokoschka', *Jahrbuch der Hamburger Kunstsammlungen* 25 (1980), p. 11.

2 Oskar Kokoschka, 'Vom Bewusstsein der Gesichte', *Genius* 1, book 1 (1919), p. 41.

3 Ibid., p. 45. The self-portraits mentioned and/or illustrated in the text are: *Double Portrait (Oskar Kokoschka and Alma Mahler)* (detail) (fig. 8, p. 215); *Self-Portrait, Hand on Chest*, 1913, oil on canvas, 79.1 x 49.5 cm, inscribed 'OK' l. r., The Museum of Modern Art, New York; *The Tempest* (detail) (plate 25); *The Knight Errant* (plate 33); *The Exiles* (whole painting and detail) (fig. 7, p. 23); and *Self-Portrait 1917*, oil on canvas, 78 x 62 cm, inscribed 'OK 1917' c. r., Von der Heydt-Museum, Wuppertal.

4 Werner Hofmann, 'Oskar Kokoschka', *Wort in der Zeit* 2, no. 3 (1956), p. 9.

5 Gombrich, 'Gedenkworte', p. 11.

6 Ibid.

7 Hans Tietze, 'Der Fall Kokoschka,' *Der Kreis* 7, no. 2 (1930), p. 81.

8 Ibid., p. 85.

9 Hofmann, 'Kokoschka', p. 9.

10 Ibid., p. 11.

11 Gombrich, 'Gedenkworte', p. 14.

12 Ben Witter, 'Mit Oskar Kokoschka rund um das Haus', *Die Zeit*, 28 July 1967.

13 *Sir Stanley Unwin*; oil on canvas, 122 x 93 cm; inscribed 'OK' l. l.; George Allen & Unwin Ltd., London.

14 The most convincing survey of Kokoschka's late painting to date was presented by Marlborough Fine Art, London, in the summer of 1990, in an exhibition of twenty-three paintings from the period 1953 to 1976. The catalogue, in English and German, includes contributions by Ernst Gombrich, Heinz Spielmann and Katharina Schulz.

15 Oskar Kokoschka, *Briefe*, ed. Olda Kokoschka and Heinz Spielmann, vol. 4, *1953-1976*, Düsseldorf, 1988, p. 235.

16 Werner Hofmann, 'Produktive Konflikte', in *Kunsthistoriker in eigener Sache: Zehn autobiographische Skizzen*, ed. Martina Sitt, Berlin, 1990, p. 124 f.

17 Oskar Kokoschka, 'Rembrandt', in idem, *Das schriftliche Werk*, vol. 3, *Aufsätze, Vorträge, Essays zur Kunst*, Hamburg, 1975, p. 111.

18 Hans M. Wingler and Friedrich Welz, *Oskar Kokoschka: Das druckgraphische Werk*, 2 vols, Salzburg, 1975, 1981; vol. 1, no. 31.

19 Ibid., no. 32.

20 Ibid., no. 61.

21 Martin Gregor-Dellin, 'Altwerden heisst, ein neues Geschäft antreten: Kunst und Radikalität in den späten Jahren', *Frankfurter Allgemeine Zeitung*, no. 103, 4 May 1985, supplement. I am grateful to Werner J. Schweiger, Vienna, for drawing my attention to this article.

22 *Shakespeare, King Lear*, 1963, Wingler and Welz, *Das druckgraphische Werk*, vol. 1, nos. 223-38; *Die Odyssee*, 1963-5, ibid., nos. 294-338; *Saul und David*, 1966-8, ibid., nos. 392-432; *Penthesilea*, 1969, ibid., nos. 454-63; *Pan*, 1975/6, ibid., vol. 2, nos. 543-60.

23 Werner Hofmann, 'The Knight Errant', in *Oskar Kokoschka 1886-1980*, exhibition catalogue, London, Tate Gallery, 1986, p. 18.

24 *Die Macht der Musik* (*Morgen und Abend*); Wingler and Welz, *Das druckgraphische Werk*, no. 366.

25 Hans Weigert, 'Kokoschka-Ausstellung in der Galerie Arnold in Dresden', *Zeitschrift für bildende Kunst* 36, nos. 11/12 (March 1925), p. 129 f.

26 Oskar Kokoschka, 'Der Expressionismus Edvard Munchs', in idem, *Aufsätze*, p. 175.

27 Henrik Ibsen, *Peer Gynt*, act 2, scene 4; quoted here in the translation by Christopher Fry, London, New York and Toronto, 1970, p. 37.

28 Ibid., act 5, scene 11; p. 167.

Plates

HMW = Hans Maria Wingler, *Oskar
       Kokoschka: The Work of the Painter*,
       Salzburg and London, 1958.
W/S = Revised and augmented *catalogue
       raisonné* of the paintings of Oskar
       Kokoschka, by Johann Winkler and
       Katharina Schulz, scheduled for
       publication at the end of 1991 by
       Verlag Galerie Welz, Salzburg. The
       dates and German titles given in the
       present book are those adopted by
       Winkler/Schulz.

Authors of the commentaries

C. B.   = Christian Bauer
I. B.   = Ingried Brugger
E. L.   = Edwin Lachnit
K. A. S. = Klaus Albrecht Schröder
K. S.   = Katharina Schulz
J. W.   = Johann Winkler

1   Girl, Hands Raised in Front of her
    Chest, 1907/8
    Mädchen, Hände vor der Brust

Oil on canvas
42 x 49 cm
Inscribed 'OK' upper left
Private collection, Vienna
HMW 1 (W/S 9)

In 1910 Kokoschka had an exhibition at the Galerie Cassirer in Berlin. Before it opened, Adolf Loos sent him a postcard commenting on a number of paintings that were under consideration for the show: 'I am definitely against your showing the "Apollo Girl". This is supposed to be a portrait exhibition, and such a painting would destroy the unity of the whole thing. The head can pass, because next to it the pictures look "beautiful".' Loos thus gives a clue as to the identity of the girl – no doubt a performer at the Apollotheater in Vienna – and confirms Hans Maria Wingler's conjecture that this was probably a half-length or full-length portrait that was cut down at a very early stage.

The work was painted in 1907/8, at the time when Kokoschka was working for the Wiener Werkstätte. In contrast to Kokoschka's contemporary graphics, with their proto-Expressionist features and their reduction to purely linear expression – as seen in numerous postcard designs and, above all, in the illustrations to the story *Die träumenden Knaben* (see fig. 8, p. 16) – it shows a compact painterly structure with an emphasis on solidity. Both the posture and the turn of the head, as well as the model's physical type, betray the influence of Ferdinand Hodler, whose work had been greatly prized in Vienna since his prominent contribution to the nineteenth exhibition of the Vienna Secession in 1904.

K.A.S.

1   Girl, Hands Raised in Front of her Chest, 1907/8

Detail of plate 1

Detail of plate 2

2 Lotte Franzos, 1909

Oil on canvas
115 x 79.5 cm
Inscribed 'OK' lower right
The Phillips Collection, Washington, D.C.
HMW 11 (W/S 34)

'Do you suppose that the person, as he or she affects me, stops short at the neck? Hair, hands, clothes, movements, are at least as important to me . . . I do not paint anatomical specimens.' With this self-justification – addressed to his client, who seems to have disliked her portrait – Kokoschka puts his finger on the salient characteristic of all his early protraiture: the way in which the inner life shines through.

Among his early portraits of women *Lotte Franzos* is distinguished by its tenderness. The dense, physical paint in the portraits painted in 1907/8 (see plate 1) gives way to a thin, porous application of colour that is not so much a skin of paint as a stain. The support shows through, and in places it is left bare. There is no firm distinction between outlines and areas of colour, and some of the drawing has been scratched into the thin paint with the brush-handle. There is a minimum of bright colour contrast; the light, transparent tonality is held together and stabilized by the strong tones of the aura, which is blue around the body and purplish brown around the head. There is something diaphanous, even immaterial, about the bodily presence. The face is that of a frail, vaporous wraith, with added accents for eyes, eyebrows and mouth. The hands form a second focus of expression.

Lotte Franzos was one of Kokoschka's earliest and most cultivated patrons. Her house was a meeting-point for the literary and artistic avant-garde. Her incomprehension of the new qualities manifest in this painting shows all the more clearly how oblivious Kokoschka was to the expectations of his contemporaries, and to the criterion of 'beautiful painting'.

K. A. S.

58

2   Lotte Franzos, 1909

3 Martha Hirsch I, 1909

Oil on canvas
88 x 70 cm
Inscribed 'OK' lower right
Private collection, U.S.A.
HMW 6 (W/S 23)

This painting is one of those that came into being through the mediation of Adolf Loos. On leaving the Kunstgewerbeschule in the early summer of 1909, Kokoschka found a close friend and patron in Loos, who encouraged him to take up portraiture and put him in touch with Herwarth Walden, art critic and editor of *Der Sturm*, and with the dealer Paul Cassirer. Wilhelm Hirsch, a wire manufacturer from Pilsen (Plzeň), was a client of Loos's, who had designed the interior of his apartment. Kokoschka's portraits of Hirsch and of his wife Martha were probably painted in Pilsen in the second half of 1909.

Not long after it was painted, *Martha Hirsch* came into the possession of Loos. In 1923 his dire financial straits forced him to place it on commission with Otto Kallir-Nirenstein, owner of the Neue Galerie in Vienna. Fritz Wolff, the owner of the Knize drapery firm, bought it in 1930, together with most of the Kokoschkas from Loos's collection.

Also known as *Woman with Large Eyes* (*Frau mit den grossen Augen*), this portrait is typical of Kokoschka's portraiture in 1909/10, with its objective of presenting 'the transitory and fluctuating states of the psyche' and its neglect of physical presence.   K.A.S.

4 Hans and Erika Tietze, 1909
Hans und Erika Tietze

Oil on canvas
76.5 x 136.2 cm
Inscribed 'OK' lower right
The Museum of Modern Art, New York
HMW 29 (W/S 35)

The Viennese man-and-wife team of art historians, Hans Tietze (1880-1954) and Erika Tietze-Conrat (1883-1958), were friendly with Adolf Loos and figured among the early advocates of the young Kokoschka. Hans Tietze published a number of essays on the artist, including the first review of his contribution to the controversial *Hagenbund* exhibition of February 1911 (see commentary to plate 9).

Kokoschka painted the couple in the library of their house in the Viennese suburb of Heiligenstadt in December 1909. Erika Tietze later noted: 'Our desks stood together in the window; Kokoschka could see us only as silhouettes. He sat in a far corner where no light penetrated, on a three-legged cobbler's stool, holding the stretched canvas balanced on his knees with his left hand. He first painted my husband in profile, just as he saw him sitting there; when it came to my turn, I had to turn my chair to face Kokoschka, because he wanted me *en face*. The light then made a halo around my dark hair.'

This description of the sitting corresponds exactly to the composition of this double portrait. A number of elements – the profile head of Hans Tietze, his right shoulder, Erika

Tietze's upper arm – stand out sharply against the comparatively intensely coloured, radiant background; other areas, saturated with light, seem to have sunk into the coloured mass of the paint. The sitters' pale faces stand out like glowing lights; the woman's head is surrounded by a fluorescent aura. Even more strongly than in *Lotte Franzos* (plate 2) of the same year Kokoschka uses a network of nervous scratchings around the figures to evoke immaterial fields of force, which he liberates from the body outline; as a result the background is filled with tension. Another unsettling element is the relationship of the two left hands to each other; in the narrow space between them an invisible field seems to build up, creating an exchange of radiation in the absence of contact.

Even before X-rays found their way into the repertory of art through the Futurists' 'Technical Manifesto', Kokoschka devised a new motif of radiation and crackling discharges that serves, both in the Tietze portrait and in *Auguste Forel* (fig. 7, p. 15), to give visible expression to the permeability or, as also in *Still Life with Lamb and Hyacinth* (plate 9), the disintegration of matter.   I.B.

5 St Veronica with the Sudarium, 1909
Veronika mit dem Schweisstuch

Oil on canvas
119 x 80 cm
Inscribed 'OK' lower right
Szépmüvészeti Múzeum, Budapest
HMW 54 (W/S 13)

In his autobiography, *My Life*, Kokoschka assigned this work to 1911, but research has established that it was painted in 1909 – even though the dominance of red and the motif of human suffering anticipate the work of the years that followed.

The medieval saint holds the cloth on which, by a miracle, the features of Christ have imprinted themselves – a subject that inspires a composition full of tension. The drawing of the saint's head is pale and faint, and with her narrowed eyes she looks like a death-mask. The centre of the picture is occupied by the saint's slightly oversized hands; by this characteristic device Kokoschka encapsulates the action in the gesture. The gentle, cradling motion of her hands is notably at odds with the action she is meant to be performing, which is to unfold her cloth.

The stark juxtaposition of two separate vehicles of expression, face and gesture, is relieved only by the unifying influence of colour. In a variety of nuances of red this intensifies the expression. Draped over the saint's right wrist, the Sudarium reveals an outline drawing of a face with staring eyes and open lips, which supplies a second facet of human suffering alongside that of the woman who carries it. From the yellowish white of her face, remote and rapt in its grief, to the crude pink of her hands, no attempt is made to present human skin in sensuous terms. In general, colour here is not used illusionistically, to model the forms: it serves to frame and demarcate the essential motifs. Thus, the spattering of white on the surface of the painting looks like a veil, enclosing and framing the figure.   C.B.

3   Martha Hirsch I, 1909

4   Hans and Erika Tietze, 1909

5   St Veronica with the Sudarium, 1909

6 Child with Parents' Hands, 1909
Kind mit den Händen der Eltern

Oil on canvas
72 x 52 cm
Inscribed 'OK' upper left
Österreichische Galerie im Belvedere, Vienna
HMW 23 (W/S 25)

In his autobiography Kokoschka says of this painting: 'The tailor Goldmann, who a few years later was to kit me out for the war, commissioned me to paint his child, then only a few weeks old. It was the Goldmanns' first child, they were happy, and to show this I included both parents' hands in the picture, holding up the little creature in its white dress, its expression stoical because it did not know why it was loved so much.'

The parental joy conveyed in this passage, the security, and the love, are not really to be found in the painting itself. Kokoschka plucks the child out of its protective cocoon of childish innocence. The knowing look, the ageless features of the face, the reduction of the tiny body to a shapeless mass and the desperately groping adult hands obliterate any sense of childish sweetness. The parents' hands encompass their son's body, not protectively and solicitously, but demandingly and possessively.

This is another work that owes its existence to Adolf Loos, who started work in the summer of 1909 on the planning of the Goldmann & Salatsch building on Michaelerplatz in Vienna. Loos eventually sold the painting to Otto Kallir-Nirenstein, who took it to New York. It was purchased by the Österreichische Galerie im Belvedere in 1963.   K.A.S.

7 Les Dents du Midi, 1909/10

Oil on canvas
80 x 116 cm
Inscribed 'OK' lower right
Dr Walter Feilchenfeldt, Zurich
HMW 30 (W/S 37)

The landscape that has become known by the title *Les Dents du Midi* is actually a view of the Gramont, just north of the Dents du Midi. Kokoschka painted it while in Switzerland in the company of Loos and the latter's consumptive girl-friend, Bessie Bruce. Recalling it in his old age, he connected it with a realization basic to his understanding of landscape as a subject: 'There was the immeasurable depth of space . . . I became aware of this after Loos had said good-bye. I was afraid to be left alone. . . . Between me and the Dents du Midi was this momentous event: that something vanishes, and yet I must carry it around with me for ever. I had to resolve this conflict, restore the balance between inner and outer worlds, bring the spirit of contemplation into harmony with palpable reality. That is why I painted this picture. In it space has a psychological meaning.'

Kokoschka fashions this vital experience into a deep, wide space, flooded with cold, winter sunshine, inviting exploration by the viewer's eye.   I.B.

8 Children Playing, 1909
Spielende Kinder

Oil on canvas
72 x 108 cm
Inscribed 'OK' lower right
Wilhelm Lehmbruck-Museum der Stadt Duisburg
HMW 19 (W/S 24)

The sitters are the children of a Viennese bookseller, one Dr Stein. Kokoschka's relationship with the Stein family is also documented by a portrait of the father, painted a short time previously.

In 1911 *Children Playing* was to be seen in the scandalous *Hagenbund* exhibition (see commentary to plate 9) that aroused such condemnation in the conservative press. Its first owner was Kokoschka's patron, Adolf Loos, and it later found its way to the Gemäldegalerie in Dresden, where it was confiscated as 'degenerate art' by the Nazis in 1937. It was sold off for 2,000 Swiss francs in Lucerne in 1939, and finally reached Duisburg by way of Malmö.

The ostensibly idyllic brother-and-sister scene is based on an organic interpenetration of figure and ground. This is clearly apparent in the configuration of the floor, which absorbs, cradles and contains the curves of the bodies. The earthy brown that surrounds the group gives way, further out, to a zone of red in various shades.

In the area of the hands this harmony is disrupted by conflicting gestures. The boy's left hand stretches out towards the clenched fist of the girl, who turns her head away. This extends the reference far beyond the realm of brotherly and sisterly relations; it comes close to evoking the theme of unrequited love, to which Kokoschka was to turn repeatedly in the period that followed.

This composition sums up a whole realm of experience that reaches back to Kokoschka's early drawings of children. Some of the colour is very thinly applied, like watercolour, and the internal modelling of the hair and the feet is reinforced by scratches made in the paint with a sharp object.   C.B.

6   Child with Parents' Hands, 1909

7   Les Dents du Midi, 1909/10

8   Children Playing, 1909

Detail of plate 9

9   Still Life with Lamb and Hyacinth, 1910

9 Still Life with Lamb and Hyacinth, 1910

Stilleben mit Hammel und Hyazinthe

Oil on canvas
87 x 114 cm
Inscribed 'OK' lower right
Österreichische Galerie im Belvedere, Vienna
HMW 21 (W/S 45)

The dating of this picture has been the subject of some controversy; latest research indicates that it was painted in the spring of 1910. In February 1911 it was among the eleven paintings (including the present plates 2, 5, 8, 10 and 11) that Kokoschka showed at an exhibition of young artists organized by the *Hagenbund* in Vienna. The critics remarked on the 'odour of decay' that emanated from his paintings, 'the repulsive plague-sores' that he had put on display. He was recommended as a suitable person to decorate 'unmentionable places with deterrent images of syphilis and paralysis'.

The late twentieth-century viewer, who has grown up with *art informel* and Actionism, is hardly in a position to appreciate how violent a crime Kokoschka's early paintings represented against the contemporary art that went by the name of *Stilkunst*. They show none of the linear definition with which an expiring Art Nouveau sought to carry its obsolete vision into the second decade of the century, none of the religious awe with which Koloman Moser, say, sought to transform a still life of fruit into a motif fit for an altar. True, Kokoschka's still life does have symbolic con-tent, but there is an Expressionist tone to his radicalism that is diametrically opposed to the Vienna Secession aesthetic.

Here is a skinned lamb, intended perhaps for an Easter or Passover feast; be that as it may, it is a *memento mori*, an allegory of transience. Creeping beasts, the denizens of the low places of the earth, complete the sinister atmosphere. Only the white hyacinth on the right glows 'like the Eternal Light itself in the darkness', but its scent reminds the painter of an experience with death. The crudity of the symbolic language is matched by a revolution in the use of colour, which detaches itself from the shape and material presence of the object and aspires to the state of pure expression.

To know the flesh: an overwhelming impulse that led the young Kokoschka to break away from the artistic conventions of his day. In the work of a present-day artist such as Hermann Nitsch existential questioning literally becomes flesh. And, as the inevitable scatological comments show, opinion-formers, in their turn, are happy to learn from the past.

E.L.

10 Ludwig Ritter von Janikowski, 1909

Oil on canvas
60.2 x 55.2 cm
Inscribed 'OK' upper right and '14. X. 09/ Steinhof' on back of canvas
Private collection, U.S.A.
HMW 27 (W/S 27)

Janikowski was an inspector in the Ministry of Railways and a close friend of Karl Kraus, to whose circle Kokoschka had been introduced by Adolf Loos. In 1909 Janikowski's health broke down, and he gradually lost his reason. The manner of Kokoschka's early portraits was highly suited to the depiction of sick and suffering humanity; indeed, the critics described his portraits of healthy individuals in terms borrowed from pathology (as in the case of *Auguste Forel*; fig. 7, p. 15). The Janikowski portrait was painted in October 1909, when the sitter was already a patient at Steinhof, the Viennese psychiatric hospital.

The head is seen in a strict frontal view; the sunken cheeks reveal the form of the skull. There is a mad look in the eyes, and the moustache oozes over the twisted upper lip like a nasal discharge. Kokoschka has painted the hideous mask of a man in whom his contemporaries had hailed a keen intellect, great verbal gifts and exceptional artistic sensibility.

When Loos parted with this painting in 1927 it passed to the Wolff-Kniže collection.

I.B.

10   Ludwig Ritter von Janikowski, 1909

11 Conte Verona, 1910

Oil on canvas
70.6 x 58.7 cm
Inscribed 'OK' lower right
Private collection, U.S.A.
HMW 32 (W/S 41)

Kokoschka remembered the sitter as 'a little Italian, who was a passionate skater and occasionally spat blood'. His portrait of this tubercular Italian aristocrat was painted in late January or early February 1910 in the Mont Blanc sanatorium for pulmonary disorders at Leysin, to which Kokoschka had accompanied Adolf Loos and Loos's girl-friend, Bessie Bruce, who was herself tubercular. In *My Life* Kokoschka describes the patients in the sanatorium as 'like shrivelled plants, for whom even the Alpine sunshine could not do much. They set little store by my painting; to them it was a minor distraction in a succession of identical days spent awaiting a cure – or the end.'

Kokoschka endows his sitter with an immaterial, even ghostly presence, as a sign of sickness and impending death. In terms of colour, the body and the outsize head blend into the background, on which are archaic-looking signs and a dark red handprint. Around the head, and over the centre-parted hair, is a run of fine scratch-marks made with the brush. The sunken, sharp-chinned face, with blood-red accents around the eyes and mouth, seems to glow with fever. The tense hands, outlined in red, reinforce the impression of helpless suffering.

I. B.

11   Conte Verona, 1910

12 Paul Scheerbart, 1910

Oil on canvas
70 x 47 cm
Inscribed 'OK' upper right
Private collection, U.S.A.
HMW 41 (W/S 52)

Well known as a writer of utopian fantasy novels, Paul Scheerbart was a leading literary contributor to the periodical *Der Sturm*. His book *Glas-Architektur*, published by *Sturm*-Verlag, was highly influential, and he was a close friend of Herwarth Walden. Kokoschka painted him in Berlin in the second half of 1910.

This portrait makes a rewarding comparison with that of the ailing Conte Verona (plate 11), painted only a few months previously. Here Kokoschka carries to an extreme his artistic devices of the dissolution of matter, the dominance of line and drably tonal colouring. The sitter's upper torso, which occupies the whole bottom half of the painting, is no more than a suggestion, as in a sketch; the paint is sparingly applied; and there are few intermediate tones between brown and black. The brush is used to draw rather than to paint. Even so, the portrait conveys a stronger bodily presence than does that of the invalid Count. Devices that serve in that work to convey the symptoms of impending death here become the expression of a cerebral but strong-willed and life-affirming personality.   K.A.S.

12   Paul Scheerbart, 1910

13 Rudolf Blümner, 1910

Oil on canvas
80 x 57.5 cm
Inscribed 'OK' upper right
Private collection
HMW 45 (W/S 51)

Blümner, an actor who gave recitals of Expressionist poetry, worked closely with Herwarth Walden on *Der Sturm* and oversaw its financial affairs until well into the 1920s. In his autobiography Kokoschka gave the following account of the friend with whom he shared a garret during his year in Berlin, in 1910/11: 'Blümner reminded me of Don Quixote, constantly riding into battle for the cause of modern art, as championed by Walden. It was a hopeless struggle against the prejudices of the day, as hopeless as charging against windmills. And that was the way I painted him and his gestures; I also several times drew his expressive face.'

The portrait shows Blümner reciting, his gesture adding emphasis to his words. The expression of the hands and that of the face relate to each other: the concentrated gaze of the close-set eyes is matched by the expressively drawn, raised right hand; the lips are parted to speak; the clenched left fist adds force and amplitude to his words.

By contrast with his previous portraits (see plates 11, 12), Kokoschka here uses more intense, more concentrated tones, applied more thickly. Vigorous and conspicuous, the brushwork is growing in expressive significance.

K.A.S.

14 William Wauer, 1910

Oil on canvas
94 x 53.5 cm
Not inscribed
Stedelijk Museum, Amsterdam
HMW 40 (W/S 50)

William Wauer had been directing plays at the Deutsches Theater in Berlin since 1906. A friend of Herwarth Walden, he was involved with *Der Sturm* on the editorial and advertising side. This portrait was painted at about the same time as *Rudolf Blümner* (plate 13).

Kokoschka shows Wauer seated, half-length. Once more, he concentrates the sitter's personality in the face and hands. Wauer holds a pose; at the same time, his seated position and precisely defined clothes stress the specific and everyday nature of the occasion. In some ways, *William Wauer* thus anticipates

the male portraits of 1913 to 1915 (see plates 28, 29, 31), in each of which the sitter's profession or personal tastes are enshrined in some characteristic accessory.

A firm, rectilinear outline encloses forms that are internally modelled in very thin paint – as also is the background. Orange and yellow supply glowing accents. The light flesh tones are marked by a heavier, crusty impasto. This juxtaposition of contrasting painterly values is typical of Kokoschka's transitional style of 1910/11.

K.A.S.

13   Rudolf Blümner, 1910

14   William Wauer, 1910

15 Cat, 1910

15 Cat, 1910

Die Katze

Oil on canvas
46 x 69 cm
Inscribed 'OK' upper left
Private collection
HMW 42 (W/S 55)

Probably painted during Kokoschka's first stay in Berlin, and stylistically close to *Paul Scheerbart* (plate 12), this was the first painting in which Kokoschka took an animal as a subject in its own right. His only previous venture into the animal kingdom had been *Still Life with Lamb and Hyacinth* (plate 9).

Kokoschka was not to revert to painting true portraits of animals – with the intention of capturing their qualities and their individuality, like that of a human being – until his years of travel, in works mostly inspired by visits to London Zoo (see plates 56, 57).

Like other early 'portraits' – and most importantly *Auguste Forel* (fig. 7, p. 15) – *Cat* has been adduced as evidence of Kokoschka's visionary gift of precognition: it was not long before it was said that the cat bears the features of Alma Mahler, whom Kokoschka is known to have first met in 1912.   I. B.

16 Hermann Schwarzwald I, 1911

Oil on canvas
90 x 65 cm
Inscribed 'OK' upper left and 'ETATIS SUAE/ 40. A. D. 1911' on back of canvas
Staatsgalerie, Stuttgart
HMW 50 (W/S 59)

Kokoschka met Hermann Schwarzwald and his wife, Eugenie, through Adolf Loos. In 1910, and again after his return from Berlin in 1911, he was a frequent guest in their hospitable house, a popular meeting-place of Viennese society and the Viennese intelligentsia.

At the time when Kokoschka painted his portrait Schwarzwald was deputy director of the Österreichisches Handelsmuseum (Austrian Trade Museum) and a diplomat; from 1921 to 1923 he worked as a head of department at the Finance Ministry, and later sat on the board of the Anglo-Austrian Bank. Kokoschka painted two further portraits of him, in 1916 and 1924.

Kokoschka shows his forty-year-old sitter – whose age we learn from the inscription on the reverse – in a seated posture that suggests concentration, even effort. In terms of sheer colour, nothing distinguishes the dark, largely undifferentiated background from the cloth of Schwarzwald's suit; the distinction is in the brushwork. Encrusted, laden with powerful streaks of black, the brushwork defines the body, for whatever lies outside that area is thinner and more fluid. The head and hands are rendered in a dry, impasted technique, using numerous juxtaposed and superimposed dabs of paint. Where the early portraits had tended towards transparency, Kokoschka had now come to emphasize the physical substance – the *matière* – of the paint, thus anticipating the style of the years that followed.
          I. B.

16   Hermann Schwarzwald I, 1911

17 Egon Wellesz, 1911

Oil on canvas
75.5 x 68.9 cm
Inscribed 'OK' upper left
Hirshhorn Museum and Sculpture Garden, Smithsonian Institution, Washington, D.C., Gift of the Joseph H. Hirshhorn Foundation, 1966
HMW 64 (W/S 65)

Kokoschka first met the musicologist and composer Egon Wellesz in the house of Hermann and Eugenie Schwarzwald (see commentary to plate 16). Along with Alban Berg, Anton von Webern (see plate 32) and Joseph Matthias Hauer, the sitter was a member of Arnold Schoenberg's circle. In exile, after 1938, Wellesz taught at the universities of Oxford and (from 1947) Princeton; he was a leading authority on the history of Byzantine and Oriental Christian music.

The Wellesz portrait is a characteristic example of the 'opaque' style that Kokoschka used for religious subjects, as well as for portraits, in 1911 and the years that followed. The typically prismatic structure of these works was probably inspired by Italian Futurism;

Kokoschka very much admired Umberto Boccioni, the most notable of the Futurist painters. The surface is brought to life by a dynamic network of colour and line that permeates the figures and conveys something of the inner tension of the individuals portrayed. The colours are light, pearly and very dense, giving an impression of sumptuousness.

This painting was purchased by the Staatliche Gemäldegalerie, Dresden, in 1929, confiscated in the Nazi purge of 'degenerate art' in 1937 and stored in a warehouse somewhere near Berlin. At the end of the war it found its way to New York, where Joseph H. Hirshhorn bought it for his collection in 1947.

K.A.S.

17   Egon Wellesz, 1911

18   St Sebastian with Angel, 1911

Heiliger Sebastian mit Engel

Oil on canvas
70.5 x 51.5 cm
Inscribed 'OK' lower left

Private collection, Vienna (on loan to
Niederösterreichisches Landesmuseum,
Vienna)

HMW 61 (W/S 62)

This work probably marks the inception of
Kokoschka's concern with biblical themes, although some authorities, among them Hans
Maria Wingler, date it to 1912. In early Austrian Expressionism generally, the theme of
Christian martyrdom reflects an evident desire
to give expression to contemporary sufferings.
In some of their works Richard Gerstl, Egon
Schiele and Kokoschka himself intensify this
tendency still further by making the suffering
saint into a self-portrait.

Stylistically, this work is characterized by
the diffuse way in which it presents its spatial
and scenic relationships. The whole surface is
pervaded by a lively play of browns and reds,
and as a result the figures are spatially some-
what ill-defined — an impression that is reinforced by a deliberate disruption of the axial
coordinates. The figures seem to hang aslant,
as if they were weightless. The work presents
no action in any real sense of the word; it is
dominated by a note of magic, almost of
spirituality. The brushwork is broad and
fluent, eschewing clear contours and internal
modelling.   C.B.

18 St Sebastian with Angel, 1911

19 Crucifixion, 1911
Kreuzigung

Oil on canvas
55 x 68 cm
Inscribed 'OK' lower left
Private collection, Zurich
HMW 53 (W/S 74)

Kokoschka's interest in the Old Masters now led him to embark on a series of history paintings on biblical subjects. Iconographically, as *Crucifixion* clearly shows, these works enshrine a blend of tradition and innovation.

The group of Christ, Mary and John, slightly off-centre, is flanked by the buildings of Jerusalem. A fairy-tale note is introduced by the figure of the knight, who – as in a number of other works of the same period by Kokoschka – appears totally out of context, in the capacity of a messenger of salvation. Next to the etiolated figure of Christ, the Manneristic form of Mary, with her elongated face, seems to be influenced by El Greco, whose work haunts all Kokoschka's religious art. Structur-

ally, there is an equal emphasis on line and on colour. In the denser areas the orange, the red and occasionally the blue are so thickly impasted as to be almost modelled.

Additional tension is generated by a linear framework that covers the composition like a grid. This work is characterized by the way in which the grid lines coincide with areas of infilling colour. In the almost exactly contemporary paintings *Knight, Death and Angel* and *The Flight from Egypt* a network of veins pervades the entire composition; here, on the other hand, it is markedly concentrated in the centre, thus adding a dynamic emphasis.

C. B.

20 Annunciation, 1911
Verkündigung

Oil on canvas
83 x 122.5 cm
Inscribed 'OK' lower left
Museum am Ostwall, Dortmund
HMW 59 (W/S 68)

One of a succession of works on religious themes, this painting radically reinterprets its iconographical sources. The biblical narrative becomes a pretext for a tense, utterly secular scene, with an overt and powerful erotic component. Drawing water from a well, the Virgin is startled by a clearly delineated, naked angel. In an almost exactly contemporary work by Kokoschka, *Visitation*, Mary herself is shown as a large nude.

The composition is dominated by the clash between different directions of motion, as resolved in the central interplay of gestures. Couched at a slant to the landscape, the figure of the Virgin is balanced by the antithetical

figure of the angel, who turns to look away, out of the picture. This conflict between the two halves of the painting is underlined by a pointed contrast between light, pastel tones on the left and dark, earthy colours on the right. The gestures mediate between the figures and embody the central message of the work. In their rhythmic movement, they themselves become the message of Christ's conception. The whole composition is held together by a web of lines that concentrates its expressive force around the body of the angel, animating the figure like a network of veins.

C. B.

21 Freiherr von Sommaruga, 1912

Oil on canvas
100 x 60 cm
Inscribed 'OK' lower right
Karl Ernst Osthaus Museum, Hagen
HMW 66 (W/S 81)

This portrait of the actor Freiherr (that is, Baron) von Sommaruga was painted in Vienna in 1912 and reproduced in Kokoschka's *Dramen und Bilder* one year later. Celebratory and assertive, it is well-nigh unique among the early portraits in having an entirely traditional composition, with the impressively looming half-length figure turned slightly to one side. The theatrical look of the sitter's dress – in other words, the way in which he is characterized by reference to his occupation – is an echo of tendencies in nineteenth-century portraiture. The face, too, is seen com-

paratively uncritically, revealing an almost straightforward response to the sitter's charm.

All this is brought to life by the artist's idiosyncratic technique. The dominant linear grid reveals a predilection for sequences of vertical strokes, which enhance the monumental character of the work. Only in the head area does the linear structure expand to permit an effective concentration of colour. The work reveals the preference for pastel tones that marks all Kokoschka's work in the years immediately after 1910. C. B.

19   Crucifixion, 1911

Detail of plate 20

20   Annunciation, 1911

21 Freiherr von Sommaruga, 1912

22   Two Nudes, 1912

22 Two Nudes, 1912

Doppelakt: Zwei Frauen

Oil on canvas
146.5 x 82.5 cm
Inscribed 'OK' lower left
Wellesley College Museum, Wellesley, Mass.,
Gift of Professor and Mrs John McAndrew
HMW 76 (W/S 80)

This picture was probably painted early in 1912, although some authorities, including Hans Maria Wingler, date it to 1913. In a letter to Alma Mahler, Kokoschka mentioned that he had just received an offer to buy the work (*Briefe*, vol. 1, p. 55).

The work combines two full-length nudes against the fragmentary background of a city. At first sight their gestures seem to interlock, but the final impression is an additive one. The postures are angular, with no sign of a smooth, rhythmic sequence of motion. All this takes place behind a linear grid that holds the composition together and reinforces it. The image dissolves into a prismatic, all-over pattern, excluding any spatial or illusionistic context. Steeped in bright light, the image favours such colours as pink, yellow, pale blue and lime-green. These pastel tones and the fractured, crystalline structure of the work suggest the influence of Robert Delaunay.

C.B.

23 Two Nudes (The Lovers), 1913

Doppelakt: Liebespaar

Oil on canvas
163 x 97.5 cm
Inscribed 'OK' lower centre
Museum of Fine Arts, Boston, Bequest of
Mrs Sarah Reed Blodgett Platt
HMW 77 (W/S 91)

Early in 1912 Kokoschka embarked on his passionate love affair with Alma Mahler, who was seven years older than he, and whose life-story reads like a cross-section through modern German culture. She was the daughter of the landscape painter Emil Jakob Schindler; after his death another painter, Carl Moll, whose portrait Kokoschka also painted (plate 28), became her stepfather. Widowed by her first husband, Gustav Mahler, Alma went on from her affair with Kokoschka to marry the German architect Walter Gropius, founder of the Bauhaus in Weimar. Finally, divorced from Gropius, she became the wife of the poet Franz Werfel.

Kokoschka's intense relationship with his 'beloved Almili' found expression in a series of paintings, the most important of which was *The Tempest* of 1913 (plate 25). *Two Nudes (The Lovers)*, with its image of two naked figures entwined as if in a dance, is another of this group of intimate expressions of emotion. It was painted early in 1913, before the couple travelled to Italy. The faceted rendering of the bodies bears a superficial resemblance to the crystalline pictorial structure of Cubism – as mediated, in all probability, through the work of Robert Delaunay and Franz Marc, which Kokoschka had seen in *Der Sturm* exhibitions in Berlin.

E.L.

24 Landscape in the Dolomites (with Cima Tre Croci), 1913

Dolomitenlandschaft (mit der Cima Tre Croci)

Oil on canvas
79.5 x 120.3 cm
Inscribed 'OK' lower left
Professor Dr Leopold, Vienna
HMW 81 (W/S 93)

This landscape was painted in late August and early September 1913, when Kokoschka was travelling in the Dolomites with Alma Mahler. It is a view of Cima Tre Croci, a massif overlooking Lake Misurina, not far from Cortina d'Ampezzo.

In about 1913 Kokoschka's painting was overtaken by a powerful sense of drama. By comparison with *Les Dents du Midi* (plate 7), *Landscape in the Dolomites* is dramatic, rhetorical, even violent. The brushwork has become cruder; there is a heavy impasto; the whole manner has coarsened. The vigorous stripes of paint seem to have been applied with decorators' brushes. Kokoschka now abandons the bright colouring of the previous years; colour differentiation remains, but its impact is reduced. Greens and blues dominate the painting, and richness of colour in detail gives way to an overall tonality. The prismatic constructions of the previous periods, with their bright, enamel-like colours (see *Two Nudes* of 1912, plate 22), are replaced by strong, dark outlines that give a linear framework to the picture as a whole, lend it dynamism and endow it with additional spatial depth.

In March 1913, shortly before this picture was painted, Kokoschka had visited Venice. His encounter with the late sixteenth-century Venetian masters, and in particular with the dramatic colour and light effects of Tintoretto and El Greco, seems to have left its mark on the dramatic style of 1913. *Landscape in the Dolomites*, together with the slightly later *The Tempest* (plate 25) and *Still Life with Putto and Rabbit* (plate 30), marks the climax of this phase in Kokoschka's art.

I.B.

23   Two Nudes (The Lovers), 1913

24   Landscape in the Dolomites (with Cima Tre Croci), 1913

25 The Tempest, 1913

25 The Tempest, 1913

Die Windsbraut

Oil on canvas
181 x 221 cm
Not inscribed
Kunstmuseum, Basle
HMW 96 (W/S 99)

Kokoschka began this painting on 10 April 1913, on his return to Vienna from his trip to Italy with Alma Mahler, and completed it in December of that year: one year earlier than was long supposed. In June 1913 he wrote to his beloved: 'This painting must be my strongest proof, the stongest I can give you on my own behalf. This I want, and this I know, and for this I will swallow fire and take no thought of death. My dear wife will not be marrying someone in whom she can have no faith.'

The Tempest, Kokoschka's most important composition of the period before the First World War and a key work of Expressionist painting, was several times overpainted as he worked on it. A letter to Alma Mahler, written in the first half of August, describes an early state of the work: 'We are not alone, as in the picture . . . we are a dual being. But as a dual being we are truly alone, solitary, and can never again unite with the vibrations of others.'

This description recalls the central image on the third fan that he made for Alma Mahler in April 1913. The total togetherness he describes, the oneness of the couple, is not present in the finished painting. Enclosed in a shell of waves and stormclouds, the couple are set adrift on the waves of a cosmic ocean. Kokoschka gazes into the distance; the woman who sleeps on his breast has been left far behind him. There is already a sense that the relationship is doomed.

In abandoning the image of total communion, Kokoschka has also rejected the harmonizing tendency of an all-pervading line. Ambivalence of content is matched by inconsistency of form. The careful equilibrium between separation and union – maintained by clearly delineated cells of solid and space – gives way to a loud, even wild, visual language. Rich, impasted paint and agitated, swirling brushwork reveal a world of ecstatic experience in a new visionary dimension, within which Kokoschka totally alters and recombines the complex relationship between his basic pictorial structures: colour and line, spatial effect and flat plane.

A letter to Herwarth Walden, dated December 1913, records the completion of the painting: 'In my studio a large work . . . *Tristan and Isolde*, has been finished for some days now. . . . This painting will be a great event when it becomes public: my strongest and greatest work, the masterpiece of all Expressionist endeavours.'

According to Kokoschka, it was the poet Georg Trakl who gave the painting the name by which it is known: 'Trakl composed his strange poem "Die Nacht" in front of my painting, saying it over until he had it by heart: ". . . Über schwärzliche Klippen/stürzt todestrunken/die erglühende Windsbraut . . ." [. . . Over darkling crags,/drunk with death,/dashes the flaring Tempest . . .]. With his pallid hand he motioned towards the picture; he gave it the name *Die Windsbraut*.'   I.B.

26 Self-Portrait with Raised Brush, 1913

Selbstbildnis mit emporgehaltenem Pinsel

Oil on canvas
108.5 x 70.5 cm
Inscribed 'OK' upper left
Kunstsammlung Nordrhein-Westfalen, Düsseldorf
HMW 87 (W/S 95)

This painting probably dates from the second half of 1913. The abrupt stylistic contrast with *Two Nudes* (*The Lovers*) (plate 23) may be explained by the artist's trip to Italy. In March and April 1913 Kokoschka and Alma Mahler visited Venice, Naples and Pompeii. The encounter with Venetian painting left a deep impression; he particularly admired the works of

Titian and, above all, Tintoretto. *Self-Portrait with Raised Brush*, which must have been painted after his return, may be traced back to these stimuli. The palpable influence of Tintoretto appears in the tonal manner and in the flickering highlights that pick out the figure against its dark background.

E.L.

26   Self-Portrait with Raised Brush, 1913

27 Portrait of a Girl, 1913

Mädchenbildnis

Oil on canvas
67.7 x 54 cm
Inscribed 'OK' lower left

Salzburger Landessammlungen –
Rupertinum, Salzburg

HMW 82 (W/S 94)

In all probability Kokoschka painted this portrait of an unidentified girl after returning from his first visit to Venice with Alma Mahler in the spring of 1913. By comparison with the earlier portraits of children – such as *Portrait of a Boy, Jacques de Menasse* of 1911 – this painting is marked by dense modelling through colour and light, and by an increasingly solid form of painting that tends towards closed form. Propping her weight on her hands, the girl sits before an extensive landscape with a lake in the distance. A dramatic mood is evoked by the light reflections that flicker across her face and that can also be seen lighting up the sky, the waters of the lake and the landscape itself. This style, with its use of light and colour to define form, presumably owes something to Kokoschka's first encounter with the work of Tintoretto, in Venice in 1913. In *My Life* Kokoschka called Tintoretto one of his 'saints'.

K.S.

27   Portrait of a Girl, 1913

28 Carl Moll, 1913

Oil on canvas
128 x 95 cm
Inscribed 'OK' lower right
Österreichische Galerie im Belvedere, Vienna
HMW 88 (W/S 96)

This portrait of the well-known Viennese landscape and genre painter Carl Moll was painted in the autumn of 1913. In his autobiography Kokoschka recalled: 'I painted Carl Moll in his patrician residence, with its neoclassical mid-Victorian décor, on the Hohe Warte, a district favoured by the prosperous Viennese bourgeoisie. . . . Moll was no genius, but he was a cultivated man. As buyer for the long-established and respected Viennese art firm of Artaria, he was the first to bring Impressionist paintings to Vienna; they were acquired by the Moderne Galerie. He had a true eye for the quality and the content of a work of art; once he discovered an important El Greco in a little provincial chapel in Spain where it was being used as a floor mat. But for his sharp eye, the picture would have been lost.'

In this portrait Kokoschka characterizes his friend and ally as an astute and successful businessman rather than as an artist. Confident and relaxed, Moll sits before us with legs crossed and elbows on the arms of his chair. The figure is built up in energetic, almost dramatic, linear strokes. Dark outlines are juxtaposed with pale streaks that seem to catch the light. The colour scheme is the same throughout the picture, so that the dynamic movement within the figure seems to radiate outwards into space. This evokes the mental alertness and flexibility of the sitter, who remained Kokoschka's supporter and friend until he died in Vienna in 1945.

K. S.

28 Carl Moll, 1913

29 Franz Hauer, 1913

Oil on canvas
120 x 106 cm
Inscribed 'OK' upper right
Museum of Art, Rhode Island School of
Design, Providence, Georgiana Aldrich Fund
and Museum Works Appropriation
HMW 92 (W/S 98)

By contrast with the roughly contemporary portrait of Carl Moll (plate 28), that of Franz Hauer shows us a shy and sensitive personality. This impression is created by such details as the downward-sloping floor, the diagonal twist in the figure and the inconsistencies of scale: compare, for instance, the expressive, oversized hands and massive lower torso with the slight, sloping shoulders and the delicate face.

Recently discovered correspondence reveals that Kokoschka wrote to Hauer to ask permission to paint his portrait: 'I would like to paint you, because your face interests me very much, and I have long wished to paint you.' The sittings took place late in 1913 at Hauer's house in Silbergasse, Vienna XIX. Not long after, in June 1914, Hauer died of appendicitis.

Franz Hauer, the elder brother of the twelve-tone composer Josef Matthias Hauer, was the proprietor of the Griechenbeisl, a celebrated tavern in the old city of Vienna. He responded sensitively to contemporary Austrian painting and built up a significant collection of paintings by Egon Schiele, Albin Egger-Lienz and Anton Faistauer. When this portrait was painted Hauer (along with Oskar Reichel) was Kokoschka's most important patron: in 1913/14 he bought seven major works, including *Two Nudes* (plate 22) and *Albert Ehrenstein* (plate 31).

In her book on Schiele's portraits Alessandra Comini gives an interesting characterization of Hauer: 'To the neglect of his five children, left motherless since 1907, he concerned himself exclusively with covering the walls of his home and gallery with works of art, leaving the operation of the Griechenbeisl to a manager. A lonely man, isolated by his tastes from his business associates, he became the friend of other solitary men and was one of the first to champion Adolf Loos. The unspoiled sincerity and directness of Hauer must have touched responsive chords in Schiele and Kokoschka. . . . The sombre Hauer was an ideal subject for Viennese Expressionism, a movement whose adherents were predisposed towards pathos' (*Egon Schiele's Portraits*, Berkeley, Los Angeles and London, 1974, pp. 123-6).   K.S.

30 Still Life with Putto and Rabbit, 1913/14

Stilleben mit Putto und Kaninchen

Oil on canvas
90 x 120 cm
Inscribed 'OK' lower right
Kunsthaus, Zurich, Vereinigung Zürcher
Kunstfreunde
HMW 95 (W/S 100)

In an arid, rugged coastal landscape an eerie scene takes place. A wild cat, crouching as if to spring, one paw raised, turns to hiss at a terrified rabbit. The cat has interposed itself in front of a naked child on the left, who is separated from the central scene by the dead limb of a tree and a crack in the ground. The three creatures seem to be held within a magic circle; there is no telling whether the predator will pounce on the child or on the rabbit. Among the hills in the background is a red, castle-like building. It stands by a river, on which a man puts out from the bank in a boat.

This painting relates to the two other large figure compositions of 1913, *Two Nudes* (*The Lovers*) (plate 23) and *The Tempest* (plate 25), in which Kokoschka embodied the experience of his passionate affair with Alma Mahler. *Two Nudes*, in which the couple are absorbed in their dance, marks the beginning of the affair; *The Tempest* is its tumultuous climax; *Still Life with Putto and Rabbit* hints at its end.

The cat bears the features of Alma Mahler, who became pregnant by Kokoschka and had an abortion. The putto on the left probably refers to the unborn child, and the helpless rabbit seems to be Kokoschka's version of his own role in those dramatic events. 'Sad child, cat chasing mouse, fire wall, meagre springtime', was his laconic description of the work in December 1913, in a letter to Herwarth Walden in Berlin. The figure in the boat has been variously interpreted as Charon or as a vision of the Underworld. It serves to carry the weird dance of the three foreground players to the very threshold between this world and the beyond.

In his autobiography Kokoschka makes a terse and bitter reference to this episode: 'It is wrong to cut short the process of life merely from indolence. This was clearly a decisive event in my development. One must keep awake to the meaning of life and not be content to vegetate.'   K.S.

29   Franz Hauer, 1913

Detail of plate 30

30   Still Life with Putto and Rabbit, 1913/14

31 Albert Ehrenstein, 1913

Oil on canvas
120 x 80 cm
Inscribed 'OK'
Národní Galerie v Praze, Prague
HMW 90 (W/S 104)

The writer Albert Ehrenstein lived mainly in Vienna until the *Anschluss* of 1938, when he went into exile. There is much evidence of his friendship and collaboration with Kokoschka, who illustrated many of his books, including *Tubutsch* (1911) and *Mein Lied* (1931). As early as 1908 Ehrenstein wrote of Kokoschka's portrait style with shrewd insight: 'He is no butcher, but a slicer-open of souls; painting the hand and the head, he weirdly uncovers his sitter's spiritual skeleton.'

Interestingly, this feature of Kokoschka's early work, the 'unpeeling of inner structures', undergoes a transformation in the very picture of which Ehrenstein himself is the subject. Kokoschka's critical, psychological detachment is replaced here by closeness. Diagonally placed, the sitter seems to be in a relaxed, almost dreamy state. This departure from Kokoschka's distinctive approach to portraiture creates an intimate likeness, the manifesto of a friendship.

The agitated line, often broken in the drawing of the garments, is coupled with a broad, planar application of colour. This tends towards monochrome, with a clear preponderance of blue-grey. The reduced emphasis on polychromatic effects, allied with a tendency to subordinate other values to a single dominant colour, is characteristic of Kokoschka's work at this time.   C.B.

106

31   Albert Ehrenstein, 1913

32 Anton von Webern, 1914

Oil on canvas
63.3 x 48.2 cm
Not inscribed
Private collection, U.S.A.
HMW 99 (W/S 111)

The composer Anton von Webern, who was a member of Arnold Schoenberg's circle, was little valued in his own lifetime and achieved due recognition only after the Second World War. Kokoschka painted his portrait in Vienna in 1914.

Slightly off-centre, the sitter is shown in extreme, even myopic close-up. The rigid, frozen pose gives the work a severity that is supported by other compositional devices. The face is sharply modelled, especially in the brow area, and the whole head has a harsh and haggard look. The concentration on the head is reinforced by the fact that this is the only part of the work in which specific features are sharply recorded; garments and background are merely hinted at. Only the occasional fitful gleam of light loosens the pictorial structure. The colour consists of variations on yellow and brown, mixed in places with blue. The diffuse painting of the background is a common feature of Kokoschka's early portraits.   C.B.

32   Anton von Webern, 1914

33 Knight Errant, 1915
Der irrende Ritter

Oil on canvas
89.5 x 180.1 cm
Inscribed 'OK' lower right and 'OKOXOK'
on back of canvas
Solomon R. Guggenheim Museum, New York
HMW 105 (W/S 115)

In *Two Nudes* (*The Lovers*) of 1913 (plate 23) Kokoschka and Alma Mahler have their arms around each other, but their faces are turned aside and their bodies seem to skip past each other. The idyll is already disturbed, as if by a premonition of the end of the relationship; and this was to emerge with increasing clarity in *The Tempest* (plate 25), in the slightly later *Still Life with Putto and Rabbit* (plate 30) and, finally, in *Knight Errant*.

This was painted in late 1914 and early 1915, shortly before Kokoschka joined the army. It shows a man in armour – undoubtedly a self-portrait – in a 'magical landscape', as the artist himself described it in a letter written at the end of November 1915: a rugged coastline lit as if by Bengal lights and lashed by a stormy sea. A woman crouches in the background on the right; her features are those of Alma. With her cheek cupped in her left hand, she adopts the traditional pose of Melancholy. No bond exists between her and the fallen knight, and Kokoschka's desolation is symbolized by the letters 'ES', which appear above his left arm. These stand for the last words of Christ on the Cross: 'My God, my God, why hast thou forsaken me?' (*Eli, eli, lama sabachthani*, Matthew XXVII: 46). Nearby, on a withered bough, there bobs a bird with a human face. (Are its features once more those of Kokoschka?)

Now that the Tempest no longer wafts him along, the artist gazes doubtfully into the future, a forlorn but also a questing and questioning figure. Kokoschka is a knight errant whose falls reveal a tendency to vertigo, whose comportment in general is uncertain and unsettled. Dizziness is a state that we often encounter in Kokoschka's work, whether in *The Power of Music* of 1920 (plate 42) or in *The Prometheus Saga* of 1950 (see fig. 5, p. 41). It suggests not that bodily powers have been lost but that they have been transcended, in a state of trance that can end in weightlessness.

Kokoschka handles this in formal terms by using two separate viewpoints. The female figure is shown in lateral view, as are the bare trees in the background on the right, the bird, the landscape and the waves of the sea; but the knight is seen from above. The figure seems to hover, expanding the pictorial space in every direction. I. B.

33   Knight Errant, 1915

34 Princess Mechtilde Lichnowsky, 1916

Fürstin Mechtilde Lichnowsky

Oil on canvas
110 x 85 cm
Inscribed 'OK' lower left
Hradec Castle, Opava
HMW 111 (W/S 121)

This portrait of the well-known essayist and short-story writer Mechtilde Lichnowsky was painted in Berlin, during the few weeks that Kokoschka spent there in the autumn of 1916, between leaving military hospital in Vienna and entering a sanatorium in Dresden.

His drawing of Princess Lichnowsky, published in the November 1916 issue of *Der Sturm*, casts light on the genesis of this painting. In the drawing, as in a number of previous portraits of men, Kokoschka involves the sitter in an action. Seated on a stool, she is reading a letter, whose contents seem to give her food for thought; she holds the paper in her right hand, raising her left hand reflectively to her brow. In the painting Kokoschka dispenses with narrative accessories, but leaves the sitter in the same pose as in the drawing. As a result, the overt emotional content of the drawing declines into the stilted pose of a 'Woman Thinking'.

With its first signs of union between the separate artistic resources of line and colour, this work anticipates the style of the Dresden years.

I.B.

34 Princess Mechtilde Lichnowsky, 1916

35 Portrait of the Artist's Mother,
    1917

Romana Kokoschka

Oil on canvas
112 x 75 cm
Inscribed 'OK' lower left
Österreichische Galerie im Belvedere, Vienna
HMW 121 (W/S 128)

In June 1917 Kokoschka's play *Hiob* received
its premiere at the Albert-Theater in Dresden.
His mother, Maria Romana Kokoschka (1861-
1934), paid a brief visit to Dresden on that
occasion, and Kokoschka took the opportunity to embark on a portrait of her. On 2 August
he wrote to her in Vienna: 'Dear Mother, send
me your photograph as soon as the small one
is ready, and after that the enlargement too.
Then I'll quickly be able to finish your picture.'

The portrait of Romana Kokoschka was
painted immediately before *Orpheus and Eurydice* (plate 38), to which it bears a stylistic
resemblance, especially in terms of colour.
However, the surface of the paint is more agitated, built up in shorter, tightly packed dabs
of the brush, so that the woman's body, face
and hands, as well as the landscape seen
through the window, seem to break down
into innumerable amorphous units. This contrasts strangely with the strict, static construction of the painting: the sitter's upright pose,
the calmly folded hands and the window
frame that firmly articulates the background.

I. B.

35   Portrait of the Artist's Mother, 1917

36 Lady with Parrot, 1916
Dame mit Papagei

Oil on canvas
84.5 x 50.5 cm
Inscribed 'OK' lower left
Staatsgalerie, Stuttgart
HMW 108 (W/S 118)

A preparatory drawing for this work, dated 1916, is in the Nationalgalerie, Berlin. It contains the layout of the painting in outline, but a comparison between the two works mainly reveals differences. Kokoschka makes the fullest use of the potential of each medium, so that the sharply linear drawing of the sketch contrasts with the heavy, painterly impasto of the present work.

Discarding his previous tendency to use a great deal of line in the construction of his paintings, he models the forms with thickly applied paint, in organic sweeps of the brush. Forms dissolve in the many areas where his broad, flat brush takes on a life of its own and forms dense slabs of paint into near-autonomous structures. The half-length figure, seated in a tranquil posture, is thus set off by an extremely lively paint surface. This is the first manifestation of a stylistic tendency that was to reach its climax in the works of 1917, in which the concept of self-contained form is entirely abandoned.

As in other works of the period, the whole colour scheme, including pink flesh tones and a grey-brown background with a reddish rose motif, subordinates itself to a dominant tone, in this case blue-grey. The primacy of colour in this work anticipates the Dresden style of the ensuing years. C.B.

116

36   Lady with Parrot, 1916

37 Lovers with Cat, 1917
Liebespaar mit Katze

Oil on canvas
93.5 x 130.5 cm
Inscribed 'OK' lower left
Kunsthaus, Zurich
HMW 116 (W/S 126)

The sitters – the Expressionist playwright Walter Hasenclever and the actress Käthe Richter, who was appearing at the Albert-Theater in Dresden – met Kokoschka during his stay at the Sanatorium Weisser Hirsch, near Dresden, where he went to recuperate from the mental and physical ravages of war service.

In spite of the light, even vaporous colouring, and a number of idyllic touches – the couple are lounging in open country on a summer day, accompanied by a white cat – the mood is strongly marked by the disruptive elements that typify Kokoschka's treatment of relationships between men and women. The woman is isolated from the man. Lost in introspection, she turns away from him and seems to refuse him the closeness that he demands of her. The texture is dense and heavy; the restless structure and the jumpy, unevenly accented brushwork are characteristic of Kokoschka's early Dresden period.

I. B.

118

37   Lovers with Cat, 1917

38 Orpheus and Eurydice, 1917
Orpheus und Eurydike

Oil on canvas
70 x 50 cm
Inscribed 'OK' upper left
Himan Brown, New York
HMW 117 (W/S 127)

So moved was Kokoschka, during his Dresden period, by the classical myth of Orpheus and Eurydice that he used it in several forms: in a drawing and in this painting, both of 1917, and one year later in a drama. The vexed issue of the relations between the sexes, which first obtrudes itself in *Lovers with Cat* (plate 37), reappears here in an extreme form: man comes to grief through woman's sexuality.

The conflict has come to a head; the man and the woman sit apart from each other, and there is no communication between them. Fully dressed, cocooned in self-absorption, the woman is oblivious to the desperate yearning in the naked man's eyes. He has used the power of song – of the spirit – to save her from Hades; to which, overcome by the power of desire, he now loses her again. Hades already gapes wide in the background, interposing a wide, black mark of separation between the two. The dark, tonal colouring and the 'dirty' colours match the sombreness of the realm of the dead; there is nothing to suggest the blaze of colour that was to erupt in Kokoschka's paintings only shortly after this one was painted.   I. B.

38   Orpheus and Eurydice, 1917

39 Stockholm Harbour, 1917

Stockholm, Hafen

Oil on canvas
85 x 125 cm
Inscribed 'OK' lower left
Private collection, Germany
HMW 118 (W/S 129)

Painted while Kokoschka was in Stockholm for an exhibition of modern Austrian art in 1917, this was his first townscape with a raised viewpoint. It shows the view across the harbour from Strandvägen. With it Kokoschka put into effect the resolve he had made in the trenches some years before, that if he survived he would paint only from the highest viewpoints he could command. This decision was the basis of the concept of the 'cosmic landscape', which came to dominate his whole approach to landscape, and to townscape in particular.

This view of Stockholm harbour is marked by 'closeness to nature': not a detailed reproduction of seen reality but the presentation of a mood that the viewer can feel and share.

The same cool, ice-blue and white colouring prevails in both the sky and the sea, which is to say, in most of the painting. The light reflects palely from the little houses that crowd together on the waterfront, and from the boats. Clouds hang low over the harbour. The chill of a late autumn day in northern Europe is palpable.

With its strong emphasis on a harmony of blue and white, the Stockholm painting recalls the colouring of *Lovers with Cat* of the same year (plate 37), but it lacks that work's animated, even nervous painterly structure. The brushwork is flatter, and thus closer to the manner of the views of Dresden that followed (see plate 44).

I.B.

40 The Pagans, 1918/19

Die Heiden

Oil on canvas
75.5 x 126 cm
Inscribed 'OK' lower right and 'Ardinghello: Es ist wahr, daß eine Rose mehrere Düfte verraucht, wenn sie am Stocke verwelkt' (Ardinghello: It is true that a rose emits several fragrances as it withers on the stem) on back of canvas
Museum Ludwig, Cologne, Stiftung Dr Haubrich
HMW 124 (W/S 134)

Kokoschka painted *The Pagans* in the winter of 1918/19. The original inscription on the reverse reveals that it was prompted by Wilhelm Heinse's novel *Ardinghello und die glückseligen Inseln* (1787). *The Pagans* is one of a group of two-figure compositions that date from the early and middle Dresden period (others are *Lovers with Cat, Orpheus and Eurydice, The Power of Music* and *Two Girls*; plates 37, 38, 42, 46). As with *Lovers with Cat*, the models for *The Pagans* were the playwright Walter Hasenclever and the actress Käthe Richter. These two, along with other friends that Kokoschka had made during his period of recuperation at the Sanatorium Weisser Hirsch, formed a committed group of pacifist protestors against the First World War.

By contrast with *Lovers with Cat*, the technique of *The Pagans* reveals all the hallmarks of the mature Dresden style: a compact, impasted skin of paint, often applied with the palette knife; glowing, often unmixed colours; and the reduction of the motif to bold, flat areas. The outlines of the two figures, and the 'drawing' of the extreme contortions and breathless foreshortenings of their complicated poses, still afford the bodies just so much three-dimensional space as they can occupy. In the works from *The Power of Music* onwards even this minimal space is neutralized by the use of an almost 'Egyptian' figure arrangement, parallel to the picture plane.

In 1937 this painting was confiscated by the Nazis from the Dresden museum.   K.A.S.

41 Self-Portrait, Hand to Mouth, 1918/19

Selbstbildnis, Hand an den Mund gelegt

Oil on canvas
83.6 x 62.8 cm
Inscribed 'OK' upper left
Professor Dr Leopold, Vienna
HMW 125 (W/S 135)

The ecstatic love affair with Alma Mahler ended in a débâcle at the beginning of 1915. Kokoschka volunteered for war service and went to the Galician front. At the end of August he was badly wounded by a bullet, which lodged in his head, and by a bayonet wound in his lung. The Vienna papers reported his death. In 1916, after his discharge from military hospital, he was sent to the Isonzo front, in Italy, where a grenade exploded close to him and put him back in hospital. Sent to convalesce in a sanatorium in Dresden, he stayed on there after his physical

recovery and tried to secure a professorship at the Kunstakademie, which he finally acquired in 1919.

Ever since the separation from Alma, who had meanwhile married the architect Walter Gropius, his mental state had remained extremely unstable, and the combination of psychological stress, desire for escape and aversion to human company found expression in *Self-Portrait, Hand to Mouth,* which he painted in late 1918 and early 1919.

E.L.

39   Stockholm Harbour, 1917

40   The Pagans, 1918/19

41   Self-Portrait, Hand to Mouth, 1918/19

42 The Power of Music, 1920
Die Macht der Musik

Oil on canvas
100 x 151.5 cm
Not inscribed
Stedelijk Van Abbemuseum, Eindhoven
HMW 130 (W/S 141)

Painted between 1918 and 1920, this is not only one of the major works of the Dresden period but a key work in Kokoschka's whole output. Created when the artist was in his early forties, it marks a clean break in his career. Kokoschka's friend, the art historian Hans Tietze, put it very succinctly: 'Between the youth and the old man, whose lives are all their own, the mature man serves the community at large. His achievements have neither the reckless vigor of youth nor the uncompromising self-sufficiency of old age; they lack the intensely personal appeal of both; what they have is the impulse to change society.'

After the psychological individualism of the early Viennese years and the erotic fixation on Alma Mahler, the Dresden period did indeed bring more general concerns to the fore. Kokoschka's gradual physical and mental recovery was accompanied by an artistic shift towards universality of content and vividness of colour. Mental phenomena beyond the individual level must be made visible; painting must uncover the operation of immaterial forces: 'Both *The Power of Music* and *Strength and Weakness* were my titles. *Strength and Weakness*, in relation to colour: yellow, red,

orange, hot colours; blue, weakening, female colours. *The Power of Music*, derived from the motif, because the summons of the trumpet flashes yellow in the painting, which in its vast, glowing mass of colour . . . begins to stir like a living organism that is roused to action.'

Both of the original alternative titles express the mission of awakening on which the artist, like a Demiurge, is engaged. The 'power of music' makes no sense as a representational theme, except as allegorically personified by the female figure with her trumpet. Transposed into colour, the power of music presents itself as 'an inner, spiritual radiance', which casts a spell on its part-vanquished, part-mutinous recipient. He is weak, but at the same time he is gaining strength. Starting up in awe, he turns to flee, and his defensive gesture becomes one of invocation, bearing away, beyond the confines of the picture, the spiritual message he has received.

The interaction of musical and visual expression, and the confrontation between strength and weakness, were henceforth to be the creative bases of Kokoschka's work (see plate 90).

E. L.

42   The Power of Music, 1920

43 Dresden, Neustadt I, 1919

Oil on canvas
81.4 x 112.2 cm
Inscribed 'OK' lower right
Private collection
HMW 131 (W/S 140)

Kokoschka painted the first of his views of the Elbe in Dresden in autumn 1919, and with it his work acquired a second major theme, alongside portraiture: the townscape. His conception of the urban landscape emerges even more clearly from this first view of Dresden than from its prelude, *Stockholm Harbour* (plate 39), painted two years earlier. It was a conception that was to govern his work right through to the late London views.

As so often with Kokoschka, an artistic preference had a biographical foundation. Kokoschka's specific form of townscape sprang from events during the First World War: 'I wanted to escape from the filthy existence that they call a war; and I swore to myself: if I ever get out of this alive, and can paint again, I'm only ever going to stand and look out from the highest buildings or from mountains, right on the top, and see what goes on in cities, and what happens to the people who live their miserable lives in those cities. And I have kept to it: my landscapes and townscapes are always painted from the very top.'

In Europe, in the second decade of the twentieth century, images of cities bore the stamp of a number of very different artistic conceptions. To those artists who were close to the Communist Party, or who were actually members of it – such as the group *Das Junge Rheinland*, George Grosz, Otto Dix or John Heartfield – the urban scene, with its cast of characters from the dregs of society, represented the ghastly, inhuman face of Capital.

To the members of the *Brücke* and *Der Blaue Reiter*, on the other hand, the city stood for a growing sense of anonymity and alienation. To the Futurists and Orphists the city was the setting for new sensations: speed, simultaneity and salutary shock.

All these philosophical approaches to urban themes ran counter to Kokoschka's idea of the city as a natural, biological organism. In the wide-angle perspective employed by Kokoschka the urban scene and all its contracting and expanding forms became a single, mutable conglomeration, with its own processes of growth and decay, which he recorded through the fleeting, small-scale form of the brushstroke (see plates 71-3).

The present view of Dresden is that which Kokoschka saw from his studio window in the academy, looking across the Elbe to the Neustadt quarter. The strictly horizontal construction of the later Dresden views has yet to emerge. The individual dabs of colour eddy across the surface and create strong accents of movement; the bridge motif, which Kokoschka uses in later Dresden paintings as a horizontal to emphasize the rectilinear construction of the painting, is still presented here – in accordance with seen reality – as a line running into depth. The deep, lustrous blue that sets the overall effect is typical of Kokoschka's Dresden palette; it also dominates the portrait of Gitta Wallerstein, painted two years later (plate 48).

I.B.

44 Dresden, Neustadt II, 1921

Oil on canvas
59.7 x 80 cm
Inscribed 'OK' lower left
The Detroit Institute of Arts, City of Detroit Purchase
HMW 135 (W/S 145)

Six of the nine pictures of Dresden that Kokoschka painted between 1919 and 1923 are variations on the view across the river Elbe from the artist's studio to the Neustadt quarter. The narrow strip of waterfront, with its tightly packed buildings, inserts itself between the sky and the river. The lowering sky contrasts with the intense red of the shoreline, which seems to separate the city from the waters. This strip of flame abruptly disturbs

the repose of the horizontal layout; the pictorial structure seems to be touched by the psychic unrest that haunted the artist throughout his early years in Dresden.

The brilliant, rich colour of the later Dresden views is not yet apparent; a dim veil seems to be cast over the scene. Across the whole canvas blackish-brown flecks break up the areas of brightly coloured impasto.

I.B.

45 Dresden, Augustus Bridge with Steamer I, 1923

Dresden, Augustusbrücke mit Dampfboot I

Oil on canvas
69 x 95 cm
Inscribed 'OK' lower left
Marlborough International Fine Art
HMW 154 (W/S 168)

Kokoschka's Dresden work has been credited with a stylistic unity that this painting totally undermines. Painted at the end of his stay in the city, it anticipates the main stylistic features of the landscapes and townscapes of his subsequent years of travel.

In previous views of the Elbe in Dresden, the motifs had consistently been arranged parallel to the picture plane; here, the bridge operates in spatial terms as a diagonal, establishing depth. The colour has become lighter overall, and the application of paint in blocks gives way to a handling that conveys excitement, motion and pulsating life. The constant tendency in earlier Dresden views to abstract the individual motifs into static, homogene-

ous areas of colour gives way to an increased realism of detail; outline comes to the fore as a means of spatial definition. All this co-exists with the powerful sense of space that was an achievement of the Dresden years.

It was not until two years later, in the rapidly painted landscapes and townscapes of Kokoschka's travels, that he began to make consistent use of the new pictorial formula evolved in this work. The paintings of Lake Geneva and Lake Lucerne, which directly followed his departure from Dresden, have neither the linear quality nor the open, porous colour that make *Dresden, Augustus Bridge with Steamer I* look so far ahead of its time.

I.B.

43   Dresden, Neustadt I, 1919

44   Dresden, Neustadt II, 1921

45   Dresden, Augustus Bridge with Steamer I, 1923

46   Two Girls, 1921/2

Zwei Mädchen

Oil on canvas
120.5 x 80 cm
Inscribed 'OK' lower left
Private collection, U.S.A.
HMW 140 (W/S 154)

During his period as a professor in Dresden Kokoschka had the use of a large studio in the academy building on the Brühlsche Terrasse, where in the early 1920s he painted a series of large paintings in which he related two or three figures to each other, defining their solidity and their position in space exclusively through the luminosity of the colour and its careful tonal gradations.

In this painting of two girls, which originally had the alternative title *Biblical Scene*, the dark tonality, dominated by shades of green and blue, reinforces the mysterious symbolism of the scene and lends the image a deliberate ambivalence. Instead of creating the illusion of space by means of perspective, Kokoschka here creates the illusion of perspective through effects of colour. Contrapuntal alternations of chromatic intensity serve to extend the pictorial space in depth and to fill out the presence of the figures. 'My paintings are getting to be like Old Masters', Kokoschka wrote from Dresden to his parents in Vienna in the early summer of 1922. In the richness and splendour of their colour values these works recall precious tapestries or the glowing colours of Gothic stained glass.

J.W.

47   Mother and Child, 1921

Mutter und Kind

Oil on canvas
51 x 60 cm
Inscribed 'OK' upper left
Musée Jenisch, Vevey, Fondation Oskar Kokoschka
HMW 137 (W/S 148)

This little painting was the curtain-raiser to a group of works painted in 1921 and 1922 on the theme of Mother and Child, which Kokoschka extended to include that of Child and Doll. The present work long retained the title *Madonna*, and the framing of the image, the mother's look of anxious solicitude and the child's serenity are indeed reminiscent of representations of the Virgin and Child.

The reversion to Christian iconography is a recurrent feature of Kokoschka's work. In his early years the *Pietà* and *Ecce homo* motifs were the vehicles of his own personal agonies (see fig. 3, p. 47); later, and especially in time of war or social distress, he used the Mother and Child or *Pietà* themes to draw attention to the suffering of others. During the Spanish Civil War he produced the lithograph of 'La Pasionaria' carrying a starving child (fig. 2, p. 38) and a poster with the inscription 'Help the Basque Children!' (fig. 1, p. 37). After the end of the Second World War he designed a poster on which Christ leans down from the cross to comfort the starving children of Europe (fig. 28, p. 223).

K.S.

46   Two Girls, 1921/2

47   Mother and Child, 1921

48 Gitta Wallerstein, 1921

48 Gitta Wallerstein, 1921

Oil on canvas
85 x 60 cm
Inscribed 'OK' upper left
Private collection
HMW 139 (W/S 149)

This delightful portrait of ten-year-old Gitta, daughter of Kokoschka's friend, the art dealer and art historian Victor Wallerstein, is one of the best-known paintings of the Dresden period. In her memories of the many years of her friendship with Kokoschka the sitter described herself as 'a terribly shy child'; her father brought her to Kokoschka's studio and left her 'in panic-stricken terror'.

Her features reflect something of the terror she felt in that unfamiliar environment, and also a certain melancholy, underlined by the dominant blue tonality that is reflected in the child's huge eyes. There is also a trace of pertness, self-will and precocity that must have been all Gitta's own.

Gitta Wallerstein was later prima ballerina at the Berlin State Opera; when Hitler came to power in 1933 she was dismissed for being Jewish. She moved to Zurich and, in 1939, to Los Angeles. She last met Kokoschka in 1936.
K.A.S.

49 Self-Portrait at the Easel, 1922
Selbstbildnis an der Staffelei

Oil on canvas
180.5 x 110.3 cm
Inscribed 'OK' lower right
Private collection, Vienna
HMW 145 (W/S 159)

This – significantly – unfinished painting marks a crux in Kokoschka's personal and artistic development. He painted it in his studio at the Dresden academy, where he had been a professor since 1919. The Dresden years marked a turning-point in his existence (see commentary to plate 42). First there were his efforts to get over the break-up of his affair with Alma Mahler. In the aftermath of this he commissioned a craftswoman to make a life-size female doll to act as a surrogate for his lost love. To the cultural historian this idea is reminiscent of the myth of Pygmalion: the work of art that is brought to life. In fact, however, the resulting artefact (fig. 14, p. 217) was more like a forebear of those plastic proxies that a man in need can purchase today in certain specialized shops. The shock of seeing this monstrous rag doll seems to have been a salutary one: freed from his obsession, Kokoschka used the doll as a model for a number of paintings, before he opened his eyes to the world at large and confronted the new artistic tasks and challenges of landscape.

Self-Portrait at the Easel may be regarded as a retrospective expression of this learning process. The painter still turns his back on the outside world, but he no longer concentrates on his ignoble model; nor does he seem deeply absorbed in his work. In spite of the frontal pose and the full-face head, no communication takes place with the viewer; the artist's eyes see no further than the picture plane. We seem, in fact, to have come upon him at the very moment when he recognizes himself as a self-caricature and becomes aware of his own numbing mental isolation. The cell-like confinement of the space, emphasized by the high vertical format, forcefully characterizes that period of alienation from reality in which Kokoschka, by his own admission, 'could not endure the company of a living human being'.

Caught in the space bounded by the intrusive doll, the barely indicated easel, which is replaced by the edge of the painting – could there be a more vivid evocation of the loss of creativity? – and the uncomfortably close back wall, with its bar-like windows in front of which there is a table or stool that cramps the space still further, the figure is forced into agonized immobility. Outside the window, however, the Elbe and the Neustadt skyline offer themselves as a *plein air* motif. In the wake of a liberating change of mood, this motif was to inaugurate the impressive series of Kokoschka's townscapes (see plates 71-3).
E.L.

49   Self-Portrait at the Easel, 1922

50 Self-Portrait with Crossed Arms, 1923

Selbstbildnis mit gekreuzten Armen

Oil on canvas
110 x 70 cm
Inscribed 'OK' lower left
Private collection, Krefeld
HMW 156 (W/S 167)

This self-portrait was painted early in 1923, a few months before Kokoschka's abrupt departure from Dresden. It is not the only self-portrait he painted while teaching at the Dresden academy. By contrast with *Self-Portrait at the Easel* (plate 49), which the painter himself dismissed as 'The Cripple' and even wanted to eliminate from the *catalogue raisonné* of his work, this is a celebratory portrait. Kokoschka is not presenting himself as an artist or – as so often – as an outsider. The conventional suit, the rigid pose, the detachment and reserve signalled by the crossed arms, and the neutral background give the portrait something of an official look, in spite of the self-doubt expressed in the face and hands.   K. A. S.

50   Self-Portrait with Crossed Arms, 1923

Detail of plate 50

Detail of plate 51

51 Karl Kraus II, 1925

Oil on canvas

65 x 100 cm

Inscribed on back of canvas: 'Pro domo et mundo. Der Sessel auf dem Karl Kraus für dieses Bild gesessen, ist nach der letzten Sitzung auseinandergefallen am 7. Feb. 25 und musste der Tischler gerufen werden. Aus dem Schiffbruch der Welt jener, die mit Brettern oder Barrikaden vor der Stirn geboren sind, has Du eine Planke zu einem Schreibtisch geborgen. OK.' (Private and public statement. The chair on which Karl Kraus sat for this painting fell apart after the last sitting, on 7 February 1925, and the carpenter had to be sent for. From the shipwreck of the world of those who were born with wooden or barricaded heads you have salvaged a plank to make a desk. OK.)

Museum Moderner Kunst, Vienna

HMW 180 (W/S 185)

In 1909 Kokoschka had painted a portrait of Karl Kraus, the great Viennese satirist, critic of language and editor of *Die Fackel*, whom he had met through Adolf Loos. That painting was destroyed when the Wallraf-Richartz-Museum in Cologne was bombed in 1944. This second portrait was painted early in February 1925 as a replacement for the first, which Kraus had paid for, but which he and his lawyer had never been able to retrieve after the exhibition in Hagen in 1910.

Kokoschka places the sitter in the right-hand half of his markedly horizontal format. The fervently gesticulating arms and hands take up much of the space. Kraus sat for this portrait in Kokoschka's mother's house in Liebhartstal, Vienna, with Loos present; it seems that the collapse of the chair at the last sitting was caused by some fierce argument between those two. K.A.S.

51   Karl Kraus II, 1925

52   Amsterdam, K
    1925

Oil on canvas
61 x 85 cm
Inscribed 'OK' lower le
Städtische Kunsthalle,
HMW 200 (W/S 216)

53   Venice, Boats
    Venedig, Boote

Oil on canvas
75 x 95 cm
Inscribed 'OK' lower ri
Bayerische Staatsgemä
Staatsgalerie moderner
HMW 167 (W/S 179)

54   Toledo, 1925

Oil on canvas
67 x 101 cm
Inscribed 'OK' lower le
Musée Jenisch, Vevey,
Fondation Oskar Koko
HMW 195 (W/S 205)

53   Venice, Boats on the Dogana, 1924

144

54   Toledo, 1925

55 Lyons, 1927

Oil on canvas
97.1 x 130.2 cm
Inscribed 'OK' lower left
The Phillips Collection, Washington, D.C.
HMW 232 (W/S 244)

In the autumn of 1927, accompanied by Dr H. J. Lütjens of the Amsterdam branch of the Galerie Cassirer, Kokoschka set out from Venice, by way of Switzerland, for France. In Lyons, in late November and early December, he painted the view from a summer-house on the slopes above the river Saône, looking across to the city on the opposite bank, with the church of Notre-Dame de Fourvière on its hill above. The boldly precipitous silhouette of the city, the magnificent sweep of the river around it, the huge sky and the soaring gulls create a powerful sense of space, breadth and openness that conveys the pulsating life of the city more vividly than any detailed rendering.

Later, Lütjens described the genesis of this urban panorama: '[Kokoschka] had a specific idea about the city; he had read about it and formed certain notions of it in his head, and he was looking for a suitable motif. He also wanted to find premises from which he could work unobserved, and where he could leave the painting until it was finished. . . . It was a laborious painting to complete – laborious because the weather kept changing and was mostly gloomy and Novemberish. His greatest enemy, however, was a thick fog. . . . He let me see the painting every day after he stopped work. This was extremely interesting. First the rough layout, in short vertical dabs of paint, widely spaced. He always insisted that once this was properly done the picture was really there already. . . . And so the Lyons painting was shown to me at a number of stages: one day it looked very like a Cézanne, and the next day it was no longer anything like it; one day the windows were precisely fitted into the facades, and the next they could scarcely be distinguished at all. He was like a sculptor who rethinks the whole of his sculpture every day; you could feel how he was shaping the thing. On the last day, at the "finish", I looked up from the footbridge over the Saône and saw him at the window with brushes everywhere, in his left hand, in his breast pocket, in his mouth, anywhere he could find to put them. He was working feverishly with his right arm stretched straight out ahead of him, picking up a different brush every instant. Then I saw the finished picture. He was overjoyed' (Hodin, 1968, p. 276f.).

K.S.

56 Mandrill, 1926

Oil on canvas
127.5 x 102.3 cm
Not inscribed
Museum Boymans-van Beuningen, Rotterdam
HMW 215 (W/S 228)

This mandrill, whose name was George, was painted at Regent's Park Zoo in London, where Kokoschka was admitted to work before opening-time. The records show that George entered the Zoo in 1917 and stayed there until his death in 1928. 'When I painted him, I saw: "That's a wild, isolated fellow, almost my own image. Someone who wants to be alone."'

Ensconced in his landscape setting, almost like the sitter in a formal portrait, the mandrill fills nearly all the canvas. The three-quarters view and the static pose reinforce the impression of a portrait – one that encapsulates all Kokoschka's long experience of portraiture. The setting is a dramatically luxuriant jungle. Stylistically, the painting belongs to the phase of Kokoschka's work in which he returns to a more intensive formal use of line. The line itself takes on a free, playful quality, ranging from sketch-like cross-hatching to almost calligraphic sweeps. In places this linear manner extends beyond the figure into very free surface patterns. The picture is uncommonly colourful, with a multitude of distinct tones centred on green and brown.

C.B.

55   Lyons, 1927

56   Mandrill, 1926

57   Deer, 1926

57 Deer, 1926

Rehe

Oil on canvas
130 x 89 cm
Inscribed 'OK' lower left and 'OK 1926' on
back of canvas
Private collection
HMW 217 (W/S 230)

Painted in Richmond Park, London, in 1926, this animal piece was shown at Cassirer's in Berlin as early as February 1927. The deer are arranged as a decorative, monumental group. The focal area, slightly right of centre, contains a tight concentration of heads, varying in position, shape and size, and interacting to evoke a wide assortment of spatial directions. The setting is conspicuously sketchy; only a few areas in the centre are more precisely articulated. Towards the edges the brushwork seems to take on a life of its own, erupting into agitated shapes that do no more than hint at a landscape setting. In some upper parts the thinly painted line breaks up into dots. The colour is dominated by a range of reds and browns, enclosed within countless nuances of green and blue.

C.B.

58 Exodus (Col de Sfa, near Biskra), 1928

Exodus (Col de Sfa bei Biskra)

Oil on canvas
89 x 130 cm
Inscribed 'OK' lower left
Deutsche Bank, Frankfurt am Main
HMW 236 (W/S 248)

It was in 1916 that Kokoschka signed the contract with the Galerie Paul Cassirer in Berlin that assured his financial survival until 1931. Cassirer's monthly retainer made it possible for the artist to leave Dresden, and in 1925 he was given unlimited credit for travel throughout Europe, to be recouped from the proceeds of sales. In 1926 Cassirer committed suicide. His successors honoured the contract with the artist, who was by now extremely well known, and underwrote his further travel plans for Africa and the Near East.

At the beginning of 1928 Kokoschka and his companion, Dr H. J. Lütjens of the Amsterdam branch of Cassirer, sailed from Marseilles to North Africa. In February Kokoschka travelled on from his first port of call, Tunis, to Algeria. From Biskra, he had himself driven out every morning to the Col de Sfa, where he painted *Exodus*. He told his mother: 'I sit in the desert and paint. . . . Now and then caravans come past, and I shall put them into the painting. With their animals, camels and sheep, they are slowly moving up into the mountains, because in the south, where the real desert is, it is already boiling hot.'

He suggestively captures the endless formlessness and monotony of the barren landscape under a blazing sun. Three caravans move along different tracks; beyond them the desert stretches away to the horizon, bounded on the right by a distant range of bleak hills. The human beings and animals in the Bedouin caravans seem drained, worn away by the sun's heat. Kokoschka sets them amid the all-devouring desert like matchstick figures, wraiths of animate beings.

I.B.

59 Market in Tunis, 1928

Markt in Tunis

Oil on canvas
86 x 128 cm
Not inscribed
Courtauld Institute Galleries, London
HMW 233 (W/S 245)

Market in Tunis is an example of the rapidly executed paintings done for the Galerie Cassirer during Kokoschka's years of travel: a mode of working that perfectly suited the quick, nervous brushwork of that period.

It seems that this painting was almost finished when the painter's vantage-point – the roof of a greengrocer's shop – collapsed in a rainstorm. In the upper part of the dominant central complex of buildings there are signs of inconsistency and haste that do not appear elsewhere in the painting, for all the sketchiness of the execution. Ultimately, this spontaneous, agitated handling, in which everything is a hint and nothing is finished, is the secret of the way in which the throb and colour of life in the narrow, crowded streets of this North African town can be credibly translated into painting.

I.B.

58   Exodus (Col de Sfa, near Biskra), 1928

Detail of plate 59

59　Market in Tunis, 1928

60 Istanbul I, 1929

Oil on canvas
80 x 110 cm
Not inscribed
Galerie vytvarného uméni, Ostrava
HMW 243 (W/S 255)

In the spring of 1929 Kokoschka and his poet friend Albert Ehrenstein set out on a journey to Egypt and Palestine, returning by way of Istanbul. The view is a wide sweep over the Bosphorus and the old city. We gain the impression that the city goes on beyond what we see, that Kokoschka is showing us not a section of Istanbul but the whole extent of the city, and that beyond it he imagines a far larger whole.

'Here', writes Fritz Schmalenbach, 'lies the reason why Kokoschka's paintings of towns are not portraits of towns. Like his other landscapes, they are segments of the world.' Schmalenbach goes on to fit these works into the tradition of the Netherlandish and German 'cosmic landscape'. Yet the suggestive power of this painting is attained by individual artistic means: a constructed spatial depth; a soaring, indefinable viewpoint; a dense atmosphere; and an open, animated handling that lends dynamism to the surface and allows the motif to 'flow on' beyond the frame.   I.B.

60   Istanbul I, 1929

61 The Marabout of Temacine (Sidi Ahmet Ben Tidjani), 1928

Der Marabout von Temacin (Sidi Ahmet Ben Tidjani)

Oil on canvas
98.5 x 130.5 cm
Inscribed 'OK' upper left
Private collection
HMW 237 (W/S 249)

In March 1928 Kokoschka's North African journey took him to Touggourt in Algeria, where he received permission to paint Sidi Ahmet Ben Tidjani, the Marabout of Temacine, a revered holy man. The fascination that Kokoschka must have felt in this alien setting emerges from his letters home to this family: 'It's really fantastic; I'm painting a blue-black Arabian prince in his palace, in the midst of his family (men only, of course).'

He described the Marabout himself as fat and imposing, an impression that is readily evoked by this portrait. Half-length, the Marabout's bulky form sits in the centre of the painting; his massive, rounded skull, with its flat nose and fleshy lips, his grave mien, his compact outline and his static pose underline the impression that this is an important personage. The colour alternates throughout between blue and beige, firmly locking the Sheikh's figure into the background. Only the purplish-brown face and hands form a contrast. The inner structural modelling of the body is defined by a restless tissue of orange lines, transparent to the underlying colours.

Kokoschka completed this portrait at the end of the fast of Ramadan and was invited to a grand banquet in the Marabout's palace. As a particular delicacy, he was served the eye of a roasted sheep. I. B.

61   The Marabout of Temacine (Sidi Ahmet Ben Tidjani), 1928

62   Arab Women and Child, 1929

Araberinnen mit Kind

Oil on canvas
88.5 x 128 cm
Inscribed 'OK' lower right
Private collection (on loan to the Tate Gallery,
London)
HMW 246 (W/S 253)

One year before this picture was painted, an acquaintanceship with a Bedouin sheikh enabled Kokoschka to paint Arab women for the first time. That painting of two young women without their veils – a 'flirtation in Arabic', as he described it in a letter to his girl-friend, Anna Kallin – was followed in the spring of 1929 by this image of two Arab women with a small child. The shy, far-away look in their eyes has nothing in common with the coquetry of the two Bedouin girls. In their self-absorption, these women do not participate by adopting a pose; they are simply letting themselves be painted.

Kokoschka's handling had also changed in the intervening year. The restless brushstroke, thinly applied colours and areas of bare canvas that characterize the 1928 *Arab Women* and *The Marabout of Temacine* (plate 61) have given way to a denser, heavier application of paint. A broad, sweeping brushstroke creates flat areas of colour, and the tonality as a whole is brighter and more luminous.   I. B.

62   Arab Women and Child, 1929

63   Marczell von Nemes, 1928

Oil on canvas
135 x 96 cm
Not inscribed
Neue Galerie der Stadt Linz,
Wolfgang-Gurlitt-Museum, Linz
HMW 245 (W/S 250)

This portrait was painted in the early summer of 1928 near Garmisch-Partenkirchen, in Bavaria, where Nemes, a wealthy art dealer, had a castle. To Kokoschka, who was on his way from North Africa to Switzerland, his sitter represented everything he most hated in that materialistic age. On 29 May 1929 he wrote to Nemes: 'You were put out, my dear Sir, because I did not believe in your Grecos, your castles, your velvets and your mountains of lovely women, just as a child does not believe in the redness of the cherries behind the display on the stall; and, after I had done a good piece of work, you could find nothing better to do than to carp. You yourself cannot live in your own castles; which is why you are so desperate for guests to put into them.'

Stylistically, Kokoschka's monumental likeness of the Hungarian aristocrat is very close to *The Marabout of Temacine*, painted in the same year (plate 61). In both portraits Kokoschka emphasizes the weight and static bulk of the body. However, by contrast with the seated Marabout, Nemes is shown stepping forward. Even more markedly than before, the canvas is covered with dry brushstrokes in a kind of all-over pattern. A number of features, such as the right hand, are defined by nothing more than a thinly brushed outline.   K. A. S.

64   Girl with Goose in Basket, 1930
Mädchen mit Gans im Korb

Oil on canvas
101 x 74 cm
Inscribed 'OK' lower right
Marlborough International Fine Art
W/S 264

In the second half of July 1930 Kokoschka travelled from Rome to Anticoli, a small village in the Sabine Hills that was a popular summer resort for artists. Within a short time he painted a number of pictures in which he incorporated the delightful surrounding landscape: a broad view across country, with farmers at work in the fields surrounded by their cattle (*Anticoli, Harvest in the Sabine Hills*); idyllic genre scenes (*Lacemaker*); and this portrait of a peasant girl on the point of setting off for market with her valuable goose.

J. W.

65   Girl with Flowers, 1932
Mädchen mit Blumen

Oil on canvas
73 x 60 cm
Inscribed 'OK' lower left
Marlborough International Fine Art
HMW 159 (W/S 283)

In 1931 Kokoschka's international standing was impressively confirmed by two major one-man shows, in Mannheim and in Paris, and yet, despite the recognition he had received from the public, from critics and from such fellow painters as Max Liebermann, his personal situation was an extremely difficult one. The art market was stagnating in the wake of the world economic crisis of 1929, and his pictures were hardly selling at all.

Probably painted in Paris in 1932, this portrait of a girl in a dream garden, greeting the viewer with a freshly picked posy, reveals nothing of the external pressures under which the artist laboured. The strongly modelled face has an unforced sweetness and joy. In a wealth of finely nuanced, loosely applied, light colours the whole scene seems to evoke the memory of carefree days of travel.

J. W.

63   Marczell von Nemes, 1928

64   Girl with Goose in Basket, 1930

65   Girl with Flowers, 1932

66   Mother and Child (Trudl in Noh Mask), 1934

67   Trudl with Head of Athena, 1931

**66   Mother and Child
(Trudl in Noh Mask), 1934**
*Mutter und Kind
(Trudl mit 'No'-Maske)*

Oil on canvas
56.5 x 77 cm
Inscribed 'OK' lower right
Galerie Würthle, Vienna
HMW 281 (W/S 302)

Trudl Bandera, the fourteen-year-old daughter of a master chimney-sweep in Liebhartstal, the district in Vienna where Kokoschka lived, sat for the painter several times in 1931. Here she wears a Japanese Noh mask and a large straw hat and holds a small child, painted from a carved wooden Baroque angel. According to Trudl herself, during the sittings Kokoschka talked to her about his African travels and lit coloured Chinese joss sticks: 'One day he told me to put on the mask and to cradle the Baroque wooden *putto* on my lap. Like a mother with her child. And that was how he painted me' (*Kronenzeitung*, Vienna, 12 April 1986, p. 27).

This painting is based on a number of preliminary drawings, made in 1931 and 1932, in which Trudl invariably appears in the mask, sometimes with and sometimes without the straw hat, and once (plate 67) holding a head of Athena instead of the putto. In the drawings and in the painting the Noh mask takes on individual features and shows human reactions, so that it ceases to be a mask and becomes a living image, just as the Baroque putto appears in the painting as a real child. Kokoschka deliberately quoted from bygone and non-European cultures in order to create a world of imagery with a fantastic wealth of connotations.   K.S.

67   Trudl with Head of Athena, 1931
Trudl mit Kopf der Athena

Oil on canvas
90 x 61 cm
Inscribed 'OK' lower left
Private collection, Italy
HMW 259 (W/S 281)

Kokoschka liked to paint and draw Trudl in a variety of disguises, some of them exotic, and to surround her with antique and other props (see plate 66). One painting shows her with a goat in an idyllic landscape, another shows her with her sister. In this scene she sits before a terrestrial globe, like an Amazon ready for battle. On her head she wears Kokoschka's

'Rembrandt cap'; she has a fencing glove on her left hand and a rapier in her right. Her right arm rests on an Oriental carpet. To the left, almost like a patron deity, is a head of Athena. This was painted from a plaster cast that Kokoschka had ordered in 1927 from an original in the Dresden museum.

K.S.

68   Santa Margherita, Harbour, 1933
Santa Margherita, Hafen

Oil on canvas
74.3 x 92.1 cm
Inscribed 'OK'
Hirshhorn Museum and Sculpture Garden, Smithsonian Institution, Washington, D.C., Gift of the Joseph H. Hirshhorn Foundation, 1966
HMW 268 (W/S 296)

This painting dates from Kokoschka's stay in Rapallo in 1933. The view of the little town, and the topography of the coast, do not interest the painter at all. Most of the canvas is taken up by the fishing-boats that lie at anchor, unrigged, and these form the true subject of the painting. A breeze rocks the brightly coloured hulls in the water and tosses their masts in different directions; in between

is the shifting, shimmering, multi-coloured sea. This is an uncommonly animated painting that vividly conveys the cheerful atmosphere of a fishing port. The motif may owe something to the inspiration of certain works by Van Gogh on similar subjects, such as *Boats on the Beach at Les Saintes-Maries de la Mer* or *Boats on the Rhône*, both painted in 1888.

I.B.

68   Santa Margherita, Harbour, 1933

69 Still Life with Summer Flowers and Ferns, 1931

Stilleben mit Sommerblumen und Farnkraut

Oil on canvas
74 x 91.5 cm
Inscribed 'OK' lower left
Marlborough International Fine Art
HMW 255 (W/S 277)

At the beginning of September 1931 Kokoschka returned to Vienna from Paris, where he had spent the past year. In April 1931 he had terminated his contract with the Galerie Cassirer, which had proposed to cut back his monthly retainer in consequence of the catastrophic state of the economy. In spite of successful exhibitions and critical recognition, Kokoschka was short of money. It was perhaps partly with a view to producing some easily saleable motifs that he painted a number of flower pieces that autumn, including the present one.

Its chromatic range recalls that of the Trudl series (see plates 66, 67), begun during the same stay in Vienna: it is colourful, yet muted. Yellows and browns dominate, and especially in the flower arrangement and in the table-cloth there are lively, powerful tones, set off – especially in the background – by 'dirty' colours. The open handling structures the paint surface. The motif – the vase of summer flowers and fern fronds – is centrally placed and relatively small; by comparison, much space is given over to the sketched-in background. Vase and ground share a common basis in colour and brushwork. This unpretentious approach is typical of Kokoschka's flower paintings. They reveal a knowledge of Delacroix's large flower pieces, which Kokoschka would have been able to study in the Louvre.

I. B.

69   Still Life with Summer Flowers and Ferns, 1931

70   Still Life with Amaryllis, 1934
      Stilleben mit Amaryllis

Oil on canvas
73 x 60 cm
Inscribed 'OK' lower left
Private collection
HMW 280 (W/S 301)

In the November 1933 issue of the magazine *Der Wiener Kunstwanderer* Thomas Mann tellingly described Kokoschka as 'a master of exact fantasy, in whose magical work the spirit becomes nature and the real grows transparent to the spiritual'. In the context of Mann's words this flower piece, painted in Vienna in the spring of 1934, the year of civil war, draws attention to Kokoschka's gift for transcending the age-old genre tradition by taking a small motif out of the immediate domestic environment and infusing it with life-affirming joy.

During the Second World War, when Kokoschka's freedom of movement was circumscribed, he devoted much attention to drawn and watercoloured nature studies. He continued using watercolour, in particular, into his old age, painting flower pieces derived from the Far Eastern brush-and-ink tradition; he liked to joke that these – in mental terms, be it understood – were his 'five-finger exercises'.   J. W.

70   Still Life with Amaryllis, 1934

71 Prague, View from the Villa
 Kramář, 1934/5
 Prag, Blick von der Villa Kramář

Oil on canvas
90 x 121 cm
Inscribed 'OK' lower left
Národní Galerie v Praze, Prague
HMW 290 (W/S 314)

72 Prague, View of the Charles
 Bridge from the Monastery of
 the Knights of the Cross, 1934
 *Prag, Blick auf die Karlsbrücke vom
 Kreuzherrenkonvent*

Oil on canvas
90 x 116 cm
Inscribed 'OK' lower left
Národní Galerie v Praze, Prague
HMW 292 (W/S 311)

73 Prague, View from the Bank of the
 River Vltava to the Malá Strana
 and the Hradčany III, 1936
 *Prag, Blick vom Moldau-Ufer auf die
 Kleinseite und den Hradschin III*

Oil on canvas
85 x 115 cm
Inscribed 'OK' lower right
Marlborough International Fine Art
HMW 304 (W/S 325)

'I liked to paint Prague.' In Kokoschka's monumental cycle of city views, unrivalled in twentieth-century art, the Golden City stands as first among equals. The theme of urban landscape was a product of the Dresden years, in which his art moved from the analysis of the individual psyche to a universal, cosmic vision (see plate 49). The static view from the studio window was soon replaced by a restless hunt for motifs that carried the artist to the furthest bounds of Europe and beyond: from Amsterdam to Istanbul, from Toledo to Stockholm, from London to Tunis.

The painted records of these journeys have nothing to do with traditional *veduta* painting, nor with the Impressionist recording of optical impressions. Kokoschka invariably paints from a high viewpoint, combining a top view with a distant one. Below a high horizon, he compresses an all-round vista into a single dynamic perspective with two vanishing points. The urban panorama thus appears not as a view of specific topographical features but as a pulsating organism. Looping lines of force, flows of movement and fields of energy set up a constant process of contraction and expansion, which only a supreme effort can pin down on the picture plane. The universality of such a vision has its historical precedent in the 'cosmic landscape' of the late Middle Ages.

In this urban experience of Kokoschka's, Prague had a special part to play. His father was born there; his sister lived there. When Vienna, the home to which he had returned from his travels, became intolerable to him — the year 1934 witnessed both his mother's death and the bloody repression of Austrian democracy — he moved to Prague. He took

Czechoslovak citizenship and painted a portrait of the president of the republic, Tomáš G. Masaryk (fig. 27, p. 222); increasingly, both in his thoughts and in his work, he found himself grappling with the menace that emanated from Germany and overshadowed the whole of Europe.

His increasing perplexity found expression in the look of the city as he depicted it. In one of the Prágue cityscapes (not illustrated here) the Charles Bridge prolongs the horizontal shoreline of the Malá Strana, thus echoing the view of the Elbe in *Dresden, Augustus Bridge with Steamer I* (plate 45). At the right-hand and bottom edges of the painting, however, something snaps. The river Vltava seems to drop vertically out of the picture; the boat looks as if it were being swept away by a cataract.

The same happens in an even more extreme form in the view from the Monastery of the Knights of the Cross across the Vltava towards the Hradčany (plate 72). Here the bridge juts diagonally into the centre of the picture from the lower left-hand corner, dividing a passage of flat calm, above and to the left, from a plunging cascade below and to the right. This more dynamic treatment of space is matched by more acute contrasts of colour, which turn a little later, in the view from the Villa Kramář (plate 71), into a shrill red-blue chord. Compositionally, the Villa Kramář painting corresponds to the view of Lyons, painted in 1927 (plate 55). However, the gentle upward curve in *Lyons*, which starts at the bend in the river and runs over the hill, has here been transformed into a riven, stalagmitic formation, like some weathered massif of rock.

E.L.

71   Prague, View from the Villa Kramář, 1934/5

72 Prague, View of the Charles Bridge from the Monastery of the Knights of the Cross, 1934

73 Prague, View from the Bank of the River Vltava to the Malá Strana and the Hradčany III, 1936

74   Self-Portrait with Stick, 1935

75   Olda Palkovská, 1937

74 Self-Portrait with Stick, 1935
Selbstporträt mit Stock

Oil on canvas
95 x 75 cm
Not inscribed
Niederösterreichisches Landesmuseum, Vienna
HMW 295 (W/S 318)

Of the many self-portraits that Kokoschka painted in the course of his life, this is one of the stillest and most contemplative. Wearing a hat and a jacket, he has the air of a wayfarer, pausing for thought in the midst of a sunlit landscape. The look in his eyes is one of intro-spection. Despite the idyllic surroundings, the mood is melancholy.

We learn from Olda Kokoschka that this self-portrait was painted in Prague in 1935, in a period overshadowed both by the death of his mother in Vienna the previous year and by the increasingly menacing political situation. In lectures, and in articles for the *Prager Tag-blatt* and the Prague literary and artistic press,

Kokoschka warned of the ethical abyss rep-resented by the Nazi ideology and spoke out for his own humanistic ideal. In June 1935 the Czechoslovak government passed an Aliens Law that barred immigrants from all political activity. With the help of President Masaryk, Kokoschka succeeded in gaining Czechoslovak citizenship. When, in July 1937, the Nazis opened the 'Degenerate Art' exhibition in Munich, which included eight works by Kokoschka, he riposted with *Self-Portrait of a 'Degenerate Artist'* (fig. 29, p. 223), in which he stands with arms folded but with eyes alert, unbendingly erect.

K.S.

75 Olda Palkovská, 1937

Oil on canvas
90 x 67 cm
Not inscribed
Musée Jenisch, Vevey, Fondation Oskar Kokoschka
W/S 331

In the winter of 1934/5, not long after his arrival in Prague, Kokoschka visited the home of a local lawyer, K. B. Palkovský, and met his host's daughter, Olda. Years later, he wrote in his autobiography: 'She became my girl-friend. She was studying law and took a Doc-torate of Jurisprudence, which I always jok-ingly called Imprudence. She would really have preferred to be an art historian. She often called for me at my studio, and we would walk through the old gardens and parks to her parents' house, on the heights beyond the Hradčany.'

A series of chalk drawings of Olda, dating from this period, conveys a deep, tranquil affection; they are the tenderest and also the most joyous portrait drawings in Kokoschka's whole *oeuvre*. It was largely thanks to Olda's

efforts that Kokoschka succeeded in escaping to England in October 1938. They were mar-ried in London in 1941.

This painting was begun in the early sum-mer of 1935, soon after Kokoschka moved into his studio overlooking the Vltava, be-tween Charles Bridge and the National Theatre. The scene seems to take place in a paradisal garden. The young woman faces the viewer in a reserved pose, with arms crossed over her breast. In her right hand she holds a pink flower, presumably a gift from the figure who is breaking off twigs in the background – a self-portrait of Kokoschka. In the back-ground, on the left, is a horned creature, half man and half beast: this is Pan, the ruler of Arcadia.

K.S.

76 Prague – Nostalgia, 1938

Oil on canvas
56 x 76 cm
Inscribed 'OK' lower left
Lord Croft, Great Britain
HMW 314 (W/S 337)

The Munich Agreement of autumn 1938 left the way open for Hitler to march into Czecho-slovakia (see plate 79). Prague was no longer a safe haven for a political refugee. With great difficulty Olda Palkovská succeeded in getting air tickets for herself and Kokoschka. On 18 October the couple flew to London with an unfinished painting in their luggage.

It cannot have been easy for Kokoschka to leave Prague. His thoughts went back to the castle hill, so often seen and painted, and now, in exile, so inaccessible. Hardly had he arrived in London when he embarked on one last Prague view, from memory.

In painting the city as he saw it, the artistic problem had been that of space; in painting it as he remembered it, the problem was the fourth dimension, that of time. At a distance, its abrupt outlines (see plates 71-3) are trans-figured into a fairy-tale idyll, to which colour adds a touch of sentiment. Erupting space gives way to a centralized composition; the dynamic river is now an enchanted fishpond. A swan waits on the thankless shore; its pas-senger, the Knight Errant, has taken the last flight to the West. What remains is nostalgia. 'I liked being in Prague.'

E.L.

76   Prague – Nostalgia, 1938

77 Anschluss – Alice in Wonderland,
    1941/2

'Anschluss' – Alice im Wunderland

Oil on canvas
63.5 x 76.3 cm
Inscribed 'OK' lower right and 'THE
"Anschluss" by OK/1939' on back of canvas
Wiener Städtische Wechselseitige Ver-
sicherungsanstalt, Vienna (on loan to Histo-
risches Museum der Stadt Wien, Vienna)
HMW 323 (W/S 346)

Painted during the bombing of London, this
painting, like *The Red Egg* (plate 80), traces the
consequences of war back to one of its causes:
in this case the annexation (*Anschluss*) of
Austria to Hitler's Germany in March 1938.
However – like *The Red Egg*, and indeed all
Kokoschka's 'political' paintings – this is nothing so simple as a straightforward condemnation of Nazi terror: it is a scathing indictment
of the Western obtuseness that had made the
triumph of inhumanity possible. Kokoschka
was firmly persuaded that Austria and
Czechoslovakia had been driven into Hitler's
arms, and that they were the sacrificial victims
of the international policy of appeasement.
On the complex allegorical significance of this
work, see the essay 'The Power of Images' in
this volume (p. 39 f.).   E. L.

77   Anschluss – Alice in Wonderland, 1941/2

78 Polperro II, 1939

Oil on canvas
60.5 x 86 cm
Inscribed 'OK' lower left and '30 years of an emigrant's artistic wisdom/an artist's signature remains – but leaders of states bloom and fall. All? Why? – How an artist lives! gives!' on back of canvas
Tate Gallery, London
HMW 318 (W/S 341)

In the summer of 1939 Kokoschka and Olda Palkovská moved from London to Polperro in Cornwall, where they lived for a year in the house of a friend, the sculptor Uli Nimptsch, until the south coast of England was declared a prohibited area for foreigners.

At Polperro Kokoschka painted a series of watercolours and two oil paintings that show the view from the terrace of the house. The deep, curved space of the foreground is intersected by the slope that thrusts in from the

right like a massive barrier, leaving the distant view free at the left. Like the townscapes, these landscapes of Kokoschka's are constructed on an elliptical compositional scheme with two foci, 'because I have always denounced the so-called *perspective cavalière*, with its single focus. Man has two eyes'.

In 1941 this painting was presented to the Tate Gallery by Edvard Beneš, then president of the Czechoslovak government in exile in London. E.L.

79 The Crab, 1939/40
Die Krabbe

Oil on canvas
63.4 x 76.2 cm
Inscribed 'OK' lower left
Tate Gallery, London
HMW 319 (W/S 342)

This painting, too, dates from late summer 1939 and was painted at Polperro. It is a vivid example of the politicization of Kokoschka's subjects at that time, shortly after Britain's entry into the war. The point of departure was purely artistic: Kokoschka came back from a morning walk with a huge crab that he had found on the beach. Its bizarre shape attracted him, and he painted a watercolour study of it.

The oil painting that followed, however, became a direct allegory of British policy towards Czechoslovakia (see plate 80). Kokoschka identified the crab, now a fearsome monster, as the British prime minister, Neville Chamberlain, who is seen leaving Czechoslovakia (the swimmer) to drown helplessly.

E.L.

80 The Red Egg, 1940/1
Das rote Ei

Oil on canvas
61 x 76 cm
Inscribed 'OK' lower right and 'a red Egg for/Manchester – Christianity wishes kindly/OK, London, 1939, Easter/time' on back of canvas
Národní Galerie v Praze, Prague
HMW 322 (W/S 345)

In Munich, on 29 September 1938, Hitler, Mussolini, Chamberlain and the French prime minister, Edouard Daladier, signed an agreement providing for the Sudeten German areas to be ceded by Czechoslovakia to Germany. On 1 October German troops marched into the Sudetenland. This concession to German demands, together with an Anglo-German non-aggression pact and an agreement to respect existing Franco-German frontiers, was intended to halt the expansionary drive of the German Reich and to secure peace in Europe. In fact, the Czechoslovak state had been shattered, enfeebled and delivered into Hitler's hands. As early as 21 October, regardless of his own assurances that after the cession of the Sudetenland he had no further territorial ambitions, Hitler issued secret orders for 'the elimination of the Czech remnant'.

More prescient than the Western politicians, Kokoschka did not wait for this to happen. On 18 October 1938 he left Prague for England. Nor did he remain silent over the fate of his father's native country, whose citi-

zenship he had himself now acquired. In the winter of 1940, after the European crisis had inexorably turned into the Second World War, he embarked on an allegorical painting that was to unmask the British-imposed policy of appeasement as one of the causes of the war.

The Munich agreement is shown as a breakfast party, with Czechoslovakia served up to the power-hungry guests. The realistic portraits of Hitler and Mussolini are unmistakable; the cat that curls around the table-leg is identifiable – by the Napoleonic hat and cockade – as France; the British lion lies crowned and majestic, its tail curled into a £ sign, on a plinth inscribed 'In Pace MUNICH'. Czechoslovakia is a roast fowl, ready for carving, which shows unexpected signs of life and takes to its wings, laying a blood-red egg as it does so. The egg (*Ei*) is the German name of Kokoschka's adoptive country – *Tschechoslowakei* – reduced to its final syllable: smashed and unwholesome food for ravening jaws.

E.L.

78 Polperro II, 1939

79   The Crab, 1939/40

80   The Red Egg, 1940/1

81   Matterhorn I, 1947

82   Venice, Punta della Dogana with View of San Giorgio, 1948

81 Matterhorn I, 1947

Oil on canvas
76.2 x 100.4 cm
Inscribed 'OK' lower left
Private collection, England
HMW 343 (W/S 366)

Early in 1947 Kokoschka visited Switzerland for the first time in nearly twenty years and painted a succession of mountain scenes that speak of a new delight in existence. From a balcony in a small hotel on the Riffelalp, near Zermatt, in September 1947 he painted two views of the Matterhorn that are among his most impressive mountain landscapes. The mountain ridges loom powerfully out of the wooded valley. In the distance the snow-covered Matterhorn glacier towers into the sky. The forest in the foreground drops away steeply; a chasm separates the viewer from the Alpine world.

Kokoschka here reveals himself as a Romantic. The proportional exaggerations, the dramatic compression of layers of space, the use of foreground trees like staffage figures and the chiaroscuro effects are typical attributes of Romantic landscape; and here, as there, they serve to give form to a religious experience of nature. This is the tenor of a letter that Kokoschka wrote, while at work on this painting, to a Swiss lawyer friend: 'So I'm painting this dramatic mountain, which towers up into the sky out of all those glaciers and abyssal depths, and I feel like a Chinese hermit, who has left the world behind and who seeks the eternal equation between his own nothingness and the Absolute. I don't know whether I shall get the painting finished, but I had to make a start, whatever happened' (*Briefe*, vol. 3, p. 190).

K. S.

82 Venice, Punta della Dogana with View of San Giorgio, 1948

Venedig, Punta della Dogana mit Blick auf San Giorgio

Oil on canvas
65 x 90 cm
Inscribed 'OK' lower left
Giovanni Deana, Venice
HMW 350 (W/S 373)

The cultural wealth of Venice, and its combination of water and architecture, always fascinated Kokoschka. Unlike his first Venetian view, painted in 1924 (plate 53), and his numerous variations on the theme of Santa Maria della Salute, this work shows the painter intrigued by the atmosphere of water, light and air, and by the busy human life on land and on the water.

Painted in June and July 1948 from a window in the Hotel Europe & Britannia, this work shows the view across the Bacino di San Marco towards the old custom house on Punta della Dogana, with San Giorgio Maggiore in the distance. Shortly after its completion it was shown at the 24th Venice Biennale.

K. S.

83 Self-Portrait (Fiesole), 1948

Selbstbildnis (Fiesole)

Oil on canvas
65.5 x 55 cm
Inscribed 'OK' upper left
Musée Jenisch, Vevey,
Fondation Oskar Kokoschka
HMW 353 (W/S 376)

In June 1948 Olda and Oskar Kokoschka travelled from London to Venice for the Biennale, in which Kokoschka was represented by a personal show of sixteen paintings. They spent the second half of the year in Florence. Kokoschka made numerous sketches of the artistic treasures of the city, painted the cathedral and climbed the Antinori Tower at the Ponte Vecchio to paint the view across the river Arno towards the Cathedral and Palazzo Vecchio.

This self-portrait was painted at Fiesole, near Florence, in August. It shows the painter, stick in hand, 'as challenging as a Condottiere' (J. P. Hodin).

K. S.

83   Self-Portrait (Fiesole), 1948

84   Cupid and Psyche, 1955
     Amor und Psyche

Tempera on canvas
238 x 233 cm
Not inscribed
Österreichische Länderbank Aktiengesell-
schaft, Vienna
HMW 389 (W/S 413)

Kokoschka first conceived this painting, based on a story by the ancient Roman writer Apuleius, as part of *The Prometheus Saga*, the triptych that he painted in 1950 for the London home of the Austrian-born collector Antoine, Count Seilern (see fig. 5, p. 41). The Cupid and Psyche story did not, however, fit the programme of the Prometheus triptych, in which (as in *The Power of Music*; plate 42) he evoked a confrontation between strength and weakness; he was to revert to this in 1954 in the *Thermopylae* triptych for Hamburg (see fig. 6, p. 42).

Replaced in *The Prometheus Saga* by a more appropriate subject, *Cupid and Psyche* was completed as an autonomous work in 1955. Soon afterwards, it was badly damaged in transit by rail, and was restored at the Akademie der bildenden Künste in Vienna. In 1956 the Wiener Gobelin-Manufaktur worked it as a tapestry, first publicly shown at Expo 58 in Brussels. This was intended for the Vienna State Opera, but was never installed there. Together with its border, also designed by Kokoschka, the tapestry is now in the Festspielhaus, Salzburg.   E. L.

84   Cupid and Psyche, 1955

85   Storm Tide in Hamburg, 1962
      Sturmflut in Hamburg

Oil on canvas
90 x 118 cm
Inscribed 'OK' lower left
Kunsthalle, Hamburg
W/S 446

Early in February 1962 Kokoschka went to Hamburg, and he was there during the disastrous flood of 16/17 February. A few days later, in an attempt to come to terms with what happened, he painted a heap of stranded, dead and dying fish with mouths agape and blankly staring eyes; this was *Storm Tide in Hamburg*. The picture is painted in vehement, agitated brushstrokes and in shimmering colours. As so often in Kokoschka's work, a still life is an allegory: an evocation of a desperate struggle against unforeseen disaster.

K.S.

86   Large London View from Shell-
      Mex House, 1959
      *London, Blick auf die Themse vom
      Shell-Mex Building*

Oil on canvas
91.5 x 123 cm
Inscribed 'OK' lower left
Tate Gallery, London
W/S 435

A mental survey of Kokoschka's townscapes reveals a clear predilection for river views; and most of his many paintings of London show the Thames and riverside areas. This chimes with the idea of the 'cosmic landscape' that marks Kokoschka's whole approach; it also serves to structure the composition and to give it extension in depth. Furthermore, the mist that often hangs above and along rivers matches the atmospheric painting style that Kokoschka evolved during the 1950s.

In accordance with his principle of the bird's-eye view, Kokoschka painted each of these London panoramas from one of the tall buildings in the vicinity of Waterloo Bridge. In the present case he shows the view downstream from Shell-Mex House towards St Paul's Cathedral.

I.B.

87   London, Tower Bridge II, 1963

Oil on canvas
91 x 125.3 cm
Inscribed 'OK' lower right
Marlborough International Fine Art
W/S 453

It was not until a decade after the end of the war that Kokoschka reverted to London themes. Between 1954, the year in which he completed the *Thermopylae* triptych (see fig. 6, p. 42), and 1970 he painted eight large London views, which are united, across all the stylistic shifts that marked his work during that period, by a single theme: the play of vast spaces.

London, Tower Bridge II was painted in 1963. The increasingly free colouring of the early 1960s combines with an evocation of light that is particularly characteristic of contemporary London views. The motif seems shrouded in a bright, shimmering mist, in which form and texture dissolve into colour. This work lacks the deep, swirling, ellipsoidal space that so often transforms Kokoschka's high-viewpoint townscapes into evocations of the 'cosmic round'.

I.B.

85   Storm Tide in Hamburg, 1962

86   Large London View from Shell-Mex House, 1959

87   London, Tower Bridge II, 1963

88 Two Girls with Dove, 1964

Zwei Mädchen mit Taube

Oil on canvas
90 x 65 cm
Inscribed 'OK' lower left and 'OK 55 - 64
Villeneuve' on back of canvas
Marlborough International Fine Art
W / S 456

Many of Kokoschka's paintings were elaborated over a long period, with the final version as the summation of a sequence of variations, which – each overlaying and transcending the last as a stage in the evolution and metamorphosis of the original pictorial idea – are all subsumed in the final work. *Two Girls with Dove* is a fine example of this process.

It was begun in 1953 as a double portrait of Louisa and Gabriela Wartmann, the daughters of Wilhelm Wartmann, long-serving director of the Kunsthaus in Zurich. In the course of its lengthy gestation, which lasted until 1964, the portrait likeness – though still detectable in the 1956 state of the work and in a contemporary lithograph – was progressively abandoned. It captures a moment of stillness amid the flux of life; and the rapt, dreamy expression on the girls' faces, and the physical interlocking that is emphasized by the intensity of the juxtaposed colours, elevate it into an allegory of the joy of human closeness.   J. W.

88   Two Girls with Dove, 1964

89 The Rejected Lover, 1966
Der abgewiesene Liebhaber

Oil on canvas
81 x 115.5 cm
Inscribed 'OK' lower right
Private collection, Hamburg
W/S 463

This painting was prompted by Kokoschka's amusement on seeing a drawing he had done years before in Dresden. Painted at Villeneuve in 1966, the work is a wry and light-hearted treatment of the erotic attraction between the sexes – a constant motif in Kokoschka's work. The woman's size and pose mark her out as the superior being. With an imperious gesture she restrains the man's ardour and sends him forth from his bed into the open air.

K. S.

90 Morning and Evening, 1966
Morgen und Abend

Oil on canvas
100 x 130 cm
Inscribed 'OK' lower left
Kunsthaus, Zurich
W/S 466

Decades after Kokoschka painted *The Power of Music* (plate 42), he saw it again, 'and I was speechless . . . . It was truly the power of music in colour.' Succumbing to the power of his own creation, he painted a second version that, in a sense, forms a continuation of the first.

In it the protagonists have exchanged roles. The awakened youth has taken hold of the trumpet, which he blows with a will. Still crouching on the ground, and therefore completely visible, but with torso erect, he now dominates the left-hand half of the picture. His hearer is a woman, seen frontally in half-length, who marks a firm vertical closure to the painting on the right. Her spell-bound gaze is not for the viewer; the music has clearly transported her to higher spheres. Her closest relatives in Kokoschka's work are the portrait drawings of Kamilla Swoboda in *Variations on a Theme* of 1920 (see fig. 1, 2, p. 11).

In the earlier painting music supplies a motive impulse, which the ambivalent figure of the youth carries away to the right; here, by contrast, the female figure arrests that impulse and transforms it once again into the immaterial essence of spiritual energy, from which it first emerged. The power of music, the power of painting, the indivisible power of art, renews itself in an endless, cyclical process, like the unerring rhythm of the tides; and so, once more, the title is *Morning and Evening*.

E. L.

89   The Rejected Lover, 1966

Detail of plate 90

90   Morning and Evening, 1966

91 Self-Portrait, 1969

92   The Seaman's Betrothed, 1967/8

91 Self-Portrait, 1969
Selbstbildnis

Oil on canvas
90.5 x 70.4 cm
Inscribed 'OK' upper left
Private collection
(on loan to the Tate Gallery, London)
W/S 472

Kokoschka began this painting on New Year's Day 1969, a few months before his eighty-third birthday. We have it on the artist's own authority that the two diminutive figures on the left and right cost him much time and thought. The female figure who leans against his right shoulder personifies warmth and security; she protects him from the wiles of the demon who lurks close to his head on the right.

In this late self-portrait Kokoschka shows himself as a man inwardly torn. The woman and the demon symbolize the two warring sides of his nature; the turn of the head, the sceptical look and the drawn features suggest that the struggle still hangs in the balance.

The intense colour and the animated brushwork underline the inherent drama and tension of this self-portrait. The woman, in her gentle tones of pink and beige, contrasts with the fiery red demon; between the two is the massive figure of the artist, clad in vivid blue. The pyrotechnic display of flesh tones stands out from the colourful background by virtue of an extremely heavy impasto. K.A.S.

92 The Seaman's Betrothed, 1967/8
Die Seemannsbraut

Oil on canvas
99.7 x 81.2 cm
Inscribed 'OK' lower right
Marlborough International Fine Art
W/S 469

Full of the wisdom of old age, this painting tells of unfulfilled hopes and of the vainness of trying to make present happiness endure. The jovial mariner, lost in the enjoyment of his pipe – Kokoschka himself, once more – has left his girl behind to embark on another voyage in the timeless realm of the imagination. He knows that parting is painful, but he also knows that it is his destiny to seek out undiscovered shores.

In terms of painting, *The Seaman's Betrothed* impressively exemplifies the mastery with which Kokoschka, in his late style, creates a tense and self-contained harmony out of an endless profusion of minutely detailed nuances of colour. J.W.

93 The Frogs, 1968
Die Frösche

Oil on canvas
61 x 91.5 cm
Inscribed 'OK' lower right and 'Europa's Sunset 1968 Prague 23 8 68' on back of canvas
Marlborough International Fine Art
W/S 471

Shortly after the establishment of the military dictatorship in Athens in 1967, Kokoschka embarked on the preparations for his first, and most emphatically political, suite of etchings: the illustrations to *The Frogs* by Aristophanes. This painting was begun, in connection with that project, in February 1968. In Aristophanes' play, a witless chorus of frogs welcomes the heroes, the god Dionysus and his servant Xantias, to the shores of the underworld, as they descend to Hades in search of the deceased tragedian Euripides. The frogs are metaphors for the obtuse mentality that fails to distinguish truth from lies, or the extraordinary from the ordinary.

This is the scene that Kokoschka recapitulates in the painting. Two plump frogs squat moronically in the twilight beside their shallow waters and fail to notice that the sun is setting behind them. Kokoschka completed the painting in the summer of 1968; after Russian troops marched into Prague on 23 August 1968 he added on the reverse the motto 'Europa's Sunset' and the date of the invasion. K.S.

206

93   The Frogs, 1968

94 Peer Gynt, 1973

Oil on canvas
115 x 89 cm
Inscribed 'OK' lower right
Private collection
W/S 480

Kokoschka was a great admirer of the Norwegian writers Henrik Ibsen and Knut Hamsun. He took Hamsun's *Pan* as the theme of his last cycle of prints, and he chose Ibsen's Peer Gynt, a hero who never catches up with his own true self, as the subject of one of his last paintings. This shows the young Peer joyously setting off in search of life. Neither his mother, Åse, who appears in the foreground, nor the girl who loves him, Solveig, can hold him back. On the features of his mother, which are Kokoschka's own, the law of return and death is written.

Under the impact of a production of *Peer Gynt* that he saw in London during the war Kokoschka wrote to his English patron and friend Edward Beddington-Behrens: 'The unique message of the play, where it differs from all literature, is that man must love, because he dies if he is alone. This is the greatest wisdom, the only one necessary to know.'

J.W.

94   Peer Gynt, 1973

95 Time, Gentlemen, Please, 1971/2

Oil on canvas
130 x 100 cm
Inscribed 'OK' lower left
and 'TIME, gentlemen please' upper left
Tate Gallery, London
W/S 478

The traditional cry of the English pub landlord
at closing time, 'Time, gentlemen, please!',
is here taken by Kokoschka to signify the
approach of death. The painter has just
answered a knock on the door; it is Death, a
bearded ancient who steps inside with his
hands still on the door-bolt. The recipient of
the summons turns his face away; he stares
out at the viewer, startled by the suddenness
of dying.

The wild brushwork and the expressive colour are characteristic of Kokoschka's late
work. The physiognomy, too, quickly and
roughly built up in a few brushstrokes, and
overwhelmingly expressive, is a mark of the
very last period in Kokoschka's career.
Kokoschka painted this picture at the age of
eighty-five. It is his last self-portrait, and in a
sense his last word as an artist.   K. A. S.

95 Time, Gentlemen, Please, 1971/2

Chronology

Compiled by Klaus Albrecht Schröder

VIENNA, 1886-1904

1886-1904

Oskar Kokoschka is born at Pöchlarn an der Donau, Lower Austria, on 1 March 1886. His mother, Maria Romana Kokoschka (1861-1934; fig. 2), comes from a family of foresters in Lower Austria; his father, Gustav Josef Kokoschka (1840-1923; fig. 1), from a celebrated line of goldsmiths in Prague. At the time of his son Oskar's birth, however, Gustav Kokoschka is no longer working as a goldsmith but as a commercial traveller for a jewellery firm, before going on to work as a book-keeper in Vienna. Oskar is the second of four children, the others being Gustav (1885-87), Berta (1889-1960) and Bohuslav (1892-1976).

A few months after Oskar's birth, the family moves to Vienna, where he is to spend the early part of his life.

From 1895 to 1905 he attends a Staatsrealschule (secondary school). As a choirboy at the Piaristenkirche in Vienna he sits in the organ loft with a fine view of the expressive late Baroque ceiling paintings by Franz Anton Maulbertsch; he will always credit Maulbertsch with a major influence on his own work as a painter. Passes higher school certificate (Matura) in 1904 and initially intends to study chemistry.

1904-1906

In 1904 Kokoschka is awarded a state scholarship to attend the Kunstgewerbeschule (School of Arts and Crafts) attached to the Österreichisches Museum für Kunst und Industrie (this is the school now known as the Hochschule für angewandte Kunst). He embarks on his studies (see fig. 3) with the intention of becoming an art teacher. His early training is strongly influenced by the stylized linear art (*Stilkunst*) of the Vienna Secession, a progressive artistic body founded as late as 1897, some of whose leading members are on the teaching staff of the Kunstgewerbeschule. Japanese woodcuts are another major influence.

1907

Kokoschka becomes a contributing artist of the Wiener Werkstätte (Vienna Workshops), which had been founded in 1903 by Josef Hoffmann, Koloman Moser and Fritz Waerndorfer with the purpose, influenced by the Arts and Crafts movement, of promoting new design and countering historicism. His most important work for the Wiener Werkstätte is a story book with fairy-tale overtones, *Die träumenden Knaben* (The Dreaming Youths). Illustrated with eight colour lithographs (see fig. 8, p. 16), and inspired by childhood memories as well as by his unrequited love for a fellow student, the book is published in 1908 in an edition of five hundred copies. Kokoschka dedicates it to a revered elder artist, Gustav Klimt.

For the Cabaret Fledermaus, founded by the Wiener Werkstätte in 1907, he writes his first one-act play, *Sphinx und Strohmann* (Sphinx and Straw Man).

Fig. 1 The artist's father

Fig. 2 The artist's mother

Fig. 3
Kokoschka (second from right) in the life class at the Kunstgewerbeschule, Vienna; seated beside him is Anton Kolig

1908-1909

The Klimt group (a splinter group from the Secession) joins with the Wiener Werkstätte and the Kunstgewerbeschule to mount an art exhibition, the 'Kunstschau'. This gives Kokoschka his first opportunity to show his work in public; he even has a room to himself. He is the only young artist to be mentioned by name in press criticisms, alongside such established former Secessionists as Klimt himself, Koloman Moser and Josef Hoffmann. For the most part, the reviews are highly uncomplimentary, although a few critics recognize the signs of a youthful and original talent. Ludwig Hevesi dubs him a 'savage chieftain' (*Oberwildling*), thus giving birth to the myth of Kokoschka the maligned, misunderstood, precocious genius. In response Kokoschka casts himself in the role of the outcast, the *artiste maudit*, by having his head shaved (see fig. 4).

At the 'Kunstschau' he meets the architect Adolf Loos, who is to be his principal mentor in the years that follow. In the same year Loos publishes his polemic against the dishonesty of aestheticism and historical ornament, *Ornament und Verbrechen* (Ornament and Crime). Loos introduces Kokoschka to the writers Karl Kraus (fig. 5, 6) and Peter Altenberg (fig. 7) and to their circle, and secures a number of portrait commissions for him. Kokoschka's new works show a forceful rejection of the aestheticism of the Wiener Werkstätte.

In 1909 he exhibits at the 'Internationale Kunstschau', in which he sees and admires works by George Minne, Edvard Munch and Vincent van Gogh. His plays *Sphinx und Strohmann* and *Mörder Hoffnung der Frauen* (Murderer the Hope of Women) are performed in the open-air theatre attached to the 'Kunstschau'.

Fig. 5   Karl Kraus, 1908

Fig. 6   *Karl Kraus*, 1909; pen and brush and ink on paper, 29.7 x 20.6 cm. Dr Walter Feilchenfeldt, Zurich

At the end of 1909, under Loos's influence, he leaves the Kunstgewerbeschule and severs his ties with the Wiener Werkstätte. He is a frequent guest of the Viennese educationalist Dr Eugenie Schwarzwald and her husband, a senior government official, Dr Hermann Schwarzwald (see plate 16). There he meets Arnold Schoenberg, Alban Berg and Anton von Webern (see plate 32).

From the late summer of 1909 onwards he begins to find the Viennese intellectual climate unduly constricting. He writes to a friend: 'I can't bear it here any longer; everything is rigid, as if no one had ever heard the scream.' At the end of the year he goes to Switzerland with Loos.

Fig. 7   Adolf Loos and Peter Altenberg, *c.* 1909

BERLIN – VIENNA – WAR SERVICE, 1910-1917

1910

At the Mont Blanc tuberculosis sanatorium Kokoschka paints a series of 'visionary portraits' of dying patients, who include a consumptive Italian aristocrat, Conte Verona (see plate 11); he also completes the portrait of Lotte Franzos, begun the year before (plate 2).

In his magazine *Die Fackel* Karl Kraus publishes the first extended critical essay on Kokoschka's work. Loos puts Kokoschka in touch with Herwarth Walden (1878-1941), editor of the Berlin magazine *Der Sturm* and future founder of the art gallery of the same name: two institutions of the greatest importance in promoting public awareness of Expressionism, Cubism and Futurism. Kokoschka remains a contributor to *Der Sturm* until 1916, with a contract (which he does not always honour) to exhibit his work at the gallery. *Der Sturm* publishes his play *Mörder Hoffnung der Frauen*, an influential work of early

far left
Fig. 4   Kokoschka the 'savage chieftan' (left) with the painter Max Oppenheimer (seated) and the actor Ernst Reinhold, *c.* 1909

Expressionist drama, as well as his drawings, which arouse great interest in German avant-garde circles.

In March he travels to Berlin for the first time to work with Walden: 'I had arrived in the capital of the German Empire, and also at the watershed between past and future.' There he shares a garret in Walden's house with the actor Rudolf Blümner (see plate 13), maintains active contacts with fellow artists, paints portraits of friends (see plates 12, 14) and leads a frenetic, bohemian existence.

A lavish showing of Kokoschka's work at the celebrated Galerie Paul Cassirer leaves the press and the public cold. However, Karl Ernst Osthaus – director of what will one day be the Karl Ernst Osthaus Museum in Hagen – buys the first work by Kokoschka ever to enter a museum, a portrait of the Duchesse de Montesquiou. Before the end of the year Osthaus also stages Kokoschka's first ever one-man show.

1911

Kokoschka returns to Vienna. On a visit to Munich he discovers that 'my friend Oppenheimer is bringing my art to the Munich public ahead of me' and accuses Max Oppenheimer (alias MOPP) of plagiarism.

In February the *Hagenbund* association of artists organizes a showing of Kokoschka's work. It centres on twenty-five paintings and ten life drawings. The conservative press condemns Kokoschka's works as 'repulsive plague-sores' and 'the delusions of sick youth'. Deeply wounded, Kokoschka will not exhibit in Vienna again until he returns, protected by the academic laurels of a Dresden professorship, in 1924.

He paints portraits of his friends, including Hermann Schwarzwald (plate 16) and the musician Egon Wellesz (plate 17), and explores a new field of subject-matter in a number of uncommissioned paintings on religious subjects, including *Crucifixion* and *Annunciation* (plates 19, 20).

1912

Kokoschka's name becomes known abroad. His work is shown in an exhibition of modern Austrian art in Budapest, in two exhibitions of Expressionist paintings, drawings and prints at the Galerie *Der Sturm* in Berlin, and in the 'Internationale Kunstausstellung des Sonderbundes' in Cologne; this last is a principal source of his growing reputation as 'the first Viennese who can be said to possess genius' (Paul Ferdinand Schmidt in a press review).

In Vienna, at the invitation of the Akademischer Verband für Musik und Literatur, Kokoschka delivers a lecture on 'The Awareness of Visions', in which he sets out to explain the disturbing features of his early portraits in terms of paranormal, mediumistic faculties. The response is hostile, and there are noisy demonstrations.

In mid-April Kokoschka meets Alma Mahler (see fig. 8, 9), stepdaughter of the painter Carl Moll (see plate 28) and widow of Gustav Mahler. While Alma is away from Vienna he writes to her of 'last summer...when I was hounded to death...and the repulsive art dealer Cassirer told me I might as well shoot myself or have myself put away, because I was incapable of conforming to this society and too impractical to conceal the fact. And you know what I am like now. Then I was old, tired to death and almost cretinous. I no longer wanted to stand on my feet because... there was not a single person worthy to hear even one true word from my lips. And now I am the joyous, youthful god, who would delight in bearing giant burdens, only to cast them off when you come to me, my only, my eternal one' (7 May 1912).

To make money, he takes on portrait commissions that he dislikes. At the end of August he succeeds at last in signing up with an art dealer (probably Gurlitt), who guarantees him a regular monthly income.

On a visit to Germany in the autumn he renews his contacts (of some years' standing) with the artists of *Der blaue Reiter*, and the group's influence is apparent in a painting such as *Two Nudes* (plate 22).

Back in Vienna, Kokoschka takes a one-year appointment at the Kunstgewerbeschule as a teaching assistant in the 'general life drawing' course.

1913

After a lengthy illness Kokoschka finds himself in financial straits, and for a time he is unable to meet his self-imposed, lifelong commitment to support his family.

Alma Mahler agrees to marry him. In the course of the year he paints all three of his celebrated double portraits of himself and Alma, including *Two Nudes* (*The Lovers*) (plate 23). Alma has a house built on the Semmering Pass for them to live in together; they travel in Italy in March and April.

Back in Vienna, Kokoschka embarks on *The Tempest* (*Die Windsbraut*) (plate 25). Several times overpainted, this work becomes a palimpsest of successive stages in the intense relationship with Alma. Originally entitled *Tristan and Isolde*, it is described by Kokoschka as 'my strongest and greatest work, the masterpiece of all Expressionist endeavours'. The title *Die Windsbraut* is conferred on it by the poet Georg Trakl.

The censors forbid the performance of Kokoschka's *Schauspiel* (Play) on moral grounds. It is, however, published by Paul Stefan, together with *Mörder Hoffnung der Frauen* and *Sphinx und Strohmann*, in a volume devoted to the artist's plays and paintings, *Oskar Kokoschka: Dramen und Bilder*.

Kokoschka's contributions to exhibitions in Budapest, Zurich, Munich and Stuttgart make him one of the best-known Expressionists.

Fig. 8   *Double Portrait (Oskar Kokoschka and Alma Mahler)*, 1912/13; oil on canvas, 100 x 90 cm. Museum Folkwang, Essen

Fig. 9   Alma Mahler, 1909

1914-1915

In the early part of 1914 Alma is pregnant by Kokoschka, and in May she has an abortion in a Vienna clinic. He puts this experience, and his own dependency on Alma, into an allegorical painting, *Still Life with Putto and Rabbit* (plate 30), which he describes to Herwarth Walden at an early stage in its execution as follows: 'sad child, cat chasing mouse, fire wall, meagre springtime' (December 1913).

In March Kokoschka finishes the dramatic poem *Wehmann und Windsbraut* (Man of Sorrows and Tempest), which is published in 1915 under the title *Allos Makar* (Happy in a Different Way). Like the *Bach Cantata* lithographs (see fig. 4, p. 47), this work bears the mark of his relationship with Alma Mahler. He writes in his autobiography: 'She could not forget that she had been married to a world-famous conductor and composer, while I was at best notorious – and that only in Vienna – and penniless. I hated...society...became jealous of every external influence, and tried by all the means at my command to isolate her.'

On 1 August the First World War breaks out.

At the end of September Kokoschka writes to Kurt Wolff: 'If I could get some money to keep my relatives' heads above water I would volunteer for the army, because staying at home is going to be an eternal mark of shame.' A further motive for Kokoschka's enlistment as a volunteer must be the impending collapse of the love affair with Alma Mahler. In Berlin, a year later, Alma marries the architect Walter Gropius, future founder of the Bauhaus.

Kokoschka enrolls in one of the most prestigious regiments in the Austro-Hungarian army, the 15th Imperial-Royal Dragoons (see fig. 10). Torn between duty and the pains of love, Kokoschka depicts himself as a 'Knight Errant' (plate 33). January 1915 sees him embarking on his basic training at Wiener Neustadt. On 22 July he is sent to the Eastern Front and assigned to patrol duty in the east of the Ukraine. Near Lutsk, at the end of August, he is shot in the head and receives a bayonet wound in the lung. The Viennese press mistakenly announces his death.

He is taken to a field hospital at Brunn am Gebirge, near Vienna, where, still bedridden, he plans his play *Orpheus und Eurydike* – another mythic treatment of his love for Alma. In October he is moved to a military hospital in the Palais Palffy in Vienna.

In the revised edition of his celebrated book *Entwicklungsgeschichte der modernen Kunst* Julius Meier-Graefe gives Kokoschka a chapter to himself. Examples of Kokoschka's painting are shown for the first time in the U.S.A., in San Francisco.

Fig. 11   Kokoschka, Berlin, September 1916

1916

On discharge from hospital Kokoschka is declared unfit for active service for three months. Now an officer, he is sent after his recovery to inspect military hospitals, and later assigned to the army press office. In mid-July he is posted as a liaison officer to the Italo-Slovene theatre of operations, on the Isonzo Front, and escorts a party of war artists to Tolmino (Tolmin). In letters to Walden he repeatedly asks him to look out for a professorial post in an academy. At the end of August a grenade explodes near the artist, resulting in shellshock and his return to hospital in Vienna.

By 9 September he is in Berlin (see fig. 11); his work at this time includes the portrait of Princess Mechtilde Lichnowsky (plate 34). In mid-September he signs an exclusive three-year contract with Walden (see fig. 12); at the end of October he cancels this and signs another, this time with Paul Cassirer (terminated only in 1931). Cassirer guarantees him a monthly retainer of 2,500 marks in return for 25 per cent of all sale proceeds.

Beginning in the autumn, Kokoschka makes repeated efforts to secure a professorship in Dresden. However, the vacancy remains unfilled until after the end of the war. Doctor friends arrange for him to convalesce in a sanatorium, run by one Dr Teuscher, close to Dresden.

Landscape in the Dolomites (with Cima Tre Croci) (plate 24) is bought by the Staatsgalerie, Munich. *The Tempest*, shown in the fortieth *Der Sturm* exhibition in Berlin in April, arouses great public interest. In Dresden Kokoschka exhibits with the Künstlervereinigung (Artists' Association), founded in 1912.

Fig. 10   Kokoschka in the uniform of a dragoon, 1915

Fig. 12   *Herwarth Walden*, 1910; oil on canvas, 100 x 69.3 cm. Staatsgalerie, Stuttgart

DRESDEN, 1917-1923

1917

Kokoschka reworks and expands *Sphinx und Strohmann* into a new play, *Hiob* (Job), which is performed at the Galerie DADA in Zurich on 14 April. The leading parts are taken by two prominent Dadaists, Hugo Ball and Tristan Tzara. Simultaneously, the same gallery shows paintings by Kokoschka, Max Ernst, Paul Klee and Vasily Kandinsky. Ball leaves Zurich in June, and the Galerie DADA closes down. *Hiob*, together with *Mörder Hoffnung der Frauen* and *Der brennende Dornbusch* (The Burning Bush), is staged at the Albert-Theater in Dresden, with Kokoschka himself directing a cast led by Ernst Deutsch and Käthe Richter (see fig. 13).

In the painting *Lovers with Cat* (plate 37) Kokoschka depicts Richter with Walter von Hasenclever; both are members — with Deutsch, the poet Ivar von Lücken and Kokoschka himself — of a small and politically committed circle of pacifists.

At the behest of the Austrian Foreign Ministry Kokoschka takes part in an exhibition of modern Austrian art in Stockholm on the occasion of the International Peace Congress. He travels to Stockholm, though he takes an extremely jaundiced view of his own participation in the exhibition: 'All my life I have been an outsider, alone, known in my own country as an amusing fool at best; and now they think it necessary to put on a modern front for the sake of the foreign public' (to Albert Ehrenstein, Stockholm, 24 October 1917).

His love of Scandinavian writers, especially August Strindberg, Henrik Ibsen and Knut Hamsun, grows deeper. He identifies with the hero of Hamsun's novel *Pan*, Lieutenant Glahn, a discharged soldier who cannot settle into a world that is alien to him; torn between two women, he loses both and kills himself in despair. Kokoschka long continues to sign letters 'Lieutenant Glahn'. Ibsen's eternally homeless Peer Gynt is another figure who haunts Kokoschka all his life (see plate 94). The mythical figures of Orpheus and Eurydice find poetic expression in a play and in a painting (plate 38).

In October he paints *Stockholm Harbour* (plate 39), the first work in which he implements the decision, taken while he was in the trenches, to paint only from the highest available viewpoints, 'to show what is left of Europe'. Kokoschka remains in constant pain from the bayonet wound in his lung. In Vienna the physiologist Robert Bárany, a Nobel Prize winner, certifies him permanently unfit for duty. In November he returns to Dresden and at once resumes his efforts to secure the vacant professorship.

1918

Gustav Klimt dies in Vienna on 6 February. Kokoschka writes to his mother: 'I cried for poor Klimt, the only Viennese artist who had any talent and character. Now I am his successor, as I once asked of him at the "Kunst-schau", and I do not yet feel ready to take charge of that flock of lost sheep.'

In Munich Kokoschka meets the puppet-maker Hermine Moos, whom he commissions to make him 'a life-size representation of my beloved [Alma Mahler], whom I ask you to reproduce faithfully and to translate into reality with all the patience and sensuality at your command.... For me this is a vital experience, which I must embrace' (letter of 20 August 1918).

He sends her a number of drawings to give her an idea of Alma's looks. The definition of surface features — skin, hair, fingernails and the like — is basic to the specification of the doll, which he himself describes as a 'fetish' and as an 'idol'. When eventually completed (fig. 14) in March 1919, it comes as a total disappointment to him: 'The outer integument is a polar-bear pelt, which would be quite suitable to replicate a shaggy bearskin rug but never the smoothness and softness of a woman's skin.... The whole thing collapses like a bundle of rags, because not enough attention has been paid... to the materials used for stuffing it' (to Hermine Moos, 6 April 1919).

Later (probably in the summer of 1920) he concludes a heavy night's drinking with friends by consigning the ill-fated surrogate to a municipal dustcart.

Fig. 13   Ernst Deutsch and Käthe Richter in Kokoschka's play *Der brennende Dornbusch* at the Albert-Theater, Dresden, 1917

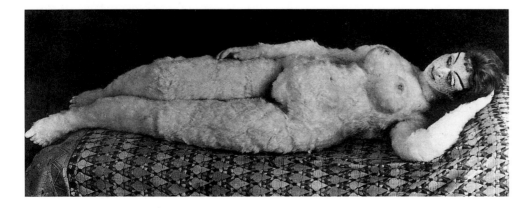

Fig. 14   The doll

On 9 November revolution breaks out in Germany. Emperor Wilhelm II abdicates, and Friedrich Ebert becomes president. On 11 November armistice on the Western Front; on 12 November the Austrian emperor, Karl, abdicates in turn.

On 3 December a group of Expressionist artists forms under the name of *Novembergruppe*: they include the sculptor Rudolf Belling, the painter Otto Dix and the architect Erich Mendelsohn. Kokoschka is in touch with the *Novembergruppe* but stays away from the founding meeting and asks for his name not to be mentioned in the press.

The first monograph on Kokoschka's work, by Paul Westheim, is published, as is an extended essay on him by the distinguished Viennese art historian Hans Tietze.

1919

In Berlin Max Reinhardt stages Kokoschka's plays *Der brennende Dornbusch* and *Hiob*.

On 18 August Kokoschka accepts a seven-year contract as a professor at the Dresden academy. The Dresden Secession, founded by Otto Dix and others, declares him an honorary member. He becomes friendly with Dr Hans Posse, the influential director of the Gemäldegalerie in Dresden, which buys his painting *The Power of Music* (plate 42).

1920

In March, in the fighting provoked by the so-called Kapp-Putsch against the newly founded Weimar Republic, a Rubens in the collection of the Zwinger in Dresden is damaged in crossfire. Kokoschka addresses an open letter to the popu'ation of Dresden: 'I request all those who intend to use firearms in order to promote their political beliefs, whether of the radical left, the radical right or the radical centre, to be kind enough to hold their military exercises elsewhere than in front of the art gallery in the Zwinger: for instance, on the shooting-ranges on the heath, where human civilization is in no danger. . . . It is certain that in future the German people will find more happiness and meaning in looking at the paintings that have been saved than in the totality of contemporary German political ideas.'

George Grosz and John Heartfield, who take a political rather than an aesthetic view of bourgeois culture, publicly denounce Kokoschka as an 'Art Thug'.

A performance of *Hiob* and *Mörder Hoffnung der Frauen* (with Heinrich George) at the Neues Theater in Frankfurt am Main on 11 April 1920 ends with fisticuffs in the auditorium and damning reviews in the press. Paul Hindemith sets *Mörder Hoffnung der Frauen* to music.

In June Kokoschka obtains leave of absence from his Dresden post and travels to Vienna, staying there for seven months. With support from his dealer, Cassirer, he buys his family a suburban house in Liebhartstal (see fig. 15).

1921

Kokoschka's lifestyle in Dresden earns him the sobriquet 'crazy Kokoschka'. He writes to his parents and brother in Vienna: 'Since leaving Vienna I have been in love about nineteen times, all serious, single-minded ladies with plenty of heart, in Frankfurt, in Berlin, and here. Wherever I go, whoever I meet, I don't let him or her leave without becoming a devotee. Then I get love letters regularly, and they are like sunshine when the sun goes in; and so I can paint wonderful colours that glow' (Dresden, late February 1921).

In February, at the Schauspielhaus in Frankfurt, Heinrich George directs the first performances of *Orpheus und Eurydike*. In June Hindemith's opera *Mörder Hoffnung der Frauen* has its premiere at the Landestheater, Stuttgart, designed and produced by Oskar Schlemmer. In Dresden Kokoschka has twenty-five paintings in the summer show of the Künstlervereinigung (see fig. 16).

1922

In April Kokoschka travels to Venice with Hans Posse to prepare for his exhibition at the Biennale. He is given a room to himself in the German pavilion and has it painted black to bring out the colours. Kokoschka's Vienna and Dresden work is presented on an equal footing with the classics of contemporary German art, Max Liebermann (see fig. 17), Max Slevogt and Lovis Corinth. After returning to Dresden in May, he writes to his father: 'I believe, in all seriousness, that I am now the best painter on earth.'

Fig. 16   *The Artist and his Muse*, 1921; poster for the Dresden Künstlervereinigung exhibition

Fig. 15
Vienna, Liebhartstal, 1924;
oil on canvas, 66 x 90 cm.
Staatliche Museen, Nationalgalerie,
Berlin (formerly GDR)

PARIS AND TRAVELS, 1923-1933

1923

Bored by the regular existence of an academy professor, Kokoschka lays plans with his girlfriend Anna Kallin to travel to Paris or to Africa: 'I hate all paintings, I hate this whole activity, I hate Europe, it's all a sham existence' (Dresden, late March 1923).

On 23 June Kokoschka is in Berlin, and in August he goes to Switzerland with Anna Kallin. The Saxon Ministry of the Interior inquires of Cassirer as to his whereabouts and discovers that he has left the country without notifying the academy. The Ministry grants him two years' leave of absence.

His father dies in Vienna on 23 October; Kokoschka spends the rest of the year in Liebhartstal with his family.

Ernst Křenek sets Orpheus und Eurydike to music.

1924

In April and May Kokoschka is in Venice: 'From the balcony of my hotel I painted the Dogana, with the silhouette of the Giudecca, from two different windows, two different angles of vision, so that I doubled the width of my visual field, an experiment I have often repeated since' (My Life).

Successful exhibitions in Berlin, Munich and Vienna. At a Vienna exhibition one painting is wantonly damaged by a visitor, and the show has to be closed. Kokoschka pens an embittered open letter: 'The incident that has taken place is...symptomatic of a sterile glorying in vandalism that runs through the whole of society; it is fed by a press hostile to creativity, which first spat venom at these same paintings in the "Kunstschau" in 1907 [recte: 1909], while the public defiled them, and which, every time I have tried to work here, in schools for children, apprentices, art students, has denounced me to the authorities.'

In October Kokoschka travels to Paris in the company of Loos and the painter Sebastian Isepp. In December he goes to Zurich, and at the end of the year to Vienna. The Kunsthalle in Hamburg purchases The Tempest (plate 25).

1925

In January Kokoschka is back in Dresden, preparing for a large retrospective at the Galerie Arnold, including forty-eight paintings and almost his complete graphic oeuvre.

Paul Cassirer grants him an unlimited credit for his intended travels around Europe, to be paid back from sales of the resulting paintings, to which Cassirer has exclusive rights.

During a stay in Vienna Kokoschka paints his second portrait of Karl Kraus (plate 51).

In company with the Frankfurt banker and art dealer Jakob Goldschmidt, Kokoschka travels to Geneva and on to Monte Carlo, Nice, Avignon and Aigues-Mortes. In March he is in Portugal, in April back in France (Bordeaux and Biarritz), returning in mid-month to Lisbon and going on to Madrid. There he is a frequent visitor to the Prado, where he admires, above all, the paintings of Velázquez. In Toledo (see plate 54) he is present at a bullfight, which he denounces (to Alice Lehmann, late April 1925) as 'a cowardly, disgusting business'.

From Madrid he writes to his mother: 'I paint a picture every ten days or so; it takes me two afternoons' (23 April 1925).

In May Kokoschka is in Paris once more, and sells all the paintings done on his tour to Cassirer and Goldschmidt. He deposits the proceeds of this first batch of travel paintings, 70,000 marks, in a Swiss bank.

He tours Holland in July and goes on to London, returning to Amsterdam (see plate 52) and thence to Switzerland; in the autumn he goes to Vienna. Everywhere he stays, he paints a townscape from a high viewpoint.

The Dresden academy asks whether Kokoschka intends to return, as his two-year sabbatical is now over. He requests another year's leave, which is granted.

In November Cassirer puts all thirty-five travel paintings on show. Meier-Graefe, in the Frankfurter Zeitung, reports seeing 'an enthusiastic crowd in front of the paintings'. The works are widely reviewed in the press. The second, expanded edition of Paul Westheim's monograph is published.

1926

On 7 January Cassirer commits suicide. Kokoschka renews his contract with Cassirer's successors, Grete Ring and Walter Feilchenfeldt. 'Here everything is in order, and it is settled that this year I am to go on another extended trip, perhaps to Egypt or somewhere, to do landscapes' (to his mother, 27 January 1926).

In spring and summer Kokoschka is in London (see fig. 18). He receives permission to paint at London Zoo outside normal opening hours; among the resulting works is Mandrill (plate 56).

In the autumn Kokoschka travels to Paris, Vienna and thence – by way of Dresden, where he once more asks for an extension of leave – to Berlin. On 27 November he is in Kassel for the premiere of Křenek's operatic version of Orpheus und Eurydike.

1927

After a flying visit to Vienna Kokoschka is in Berlin from mid-January to mid-May. Exhibitions of 'portraits of people and animals' at the Flechtheim and Cassirer galleries ('Bildnisse von Oskar Kokoschka: Menschen und Tiere') are followed by the largest retrospective show to date, at the Kunsthaus in Zurich, with 101 paintings, 49 watercolours and drawings, and 110 prints. All the major German museums have by now purchased paintings by him.

Fig. 17 *Max Liebermann*, 1923; lithograph, 80.1 x 61.1 cm

Fig. 18 Kokoschka, London, 1926

Fig. 19 Kokoschka in North Africa, 1928

Fig. 20 North African street scene; photograph by Helmuth Lütjens, 1928

The faculty board in Dresden decides to appoint a successor, 'since it seems impossible to secure binding consent from Kokoschka'. That successor is Otto Dix.

In autumn Kokoschka travels to Venice; Dr Helmuth Lütjens of the Galerie Cassirer joins him there and acts as his companion on a journey through northern Italy and Switzerland to France. In November and December Kokoschka is in Lyons (see plate 55); he then goes on to Paris. With Lütjens he plans an extended trip to North Africa.

1928
Lütjens and Kokoschka arrive in Tunis on 5 January (see fig. 19, 20). At once, perched on the roof of a greengrocer's shop, Kokoschka begins painting *Market in Tunis* (plate 59). In February he travels on to Algeria. North of Biskra he paints *Exodus* (plate 58). At Touggourt he receives permission to paint a portrait of the Marabout of Temacine (plate 61). In April he moves on, via Morocco and Gibraltar, to Spain, and in May returns to Switzerland. From June to August, and in November and December, he visits England and Ireland; in between and afterwards, he is in Vienna.

1929
Early in the year Kokoschka and his friend Albert Ehrenstein travel to Egypt and Palestine. Among other works, he paints *Arab Women and Child* (plate 62). In the summer he spends several weeks in Istanbul and paints the view across the Bosphorus to the old city (plate 60).

At the end of July he returns to Zurich by way of Athens and Venice. His depression, not eased by all this travel, causes him to write to a girl-friend, Alice Lehmann: 'The only certain thing is that I have a beginning and an end as Herr Oskar Kokoschka, and that the few nomads that still exist will meet as scabby an end as I shall, before they are kissed to sleep.... Tomorrow night I shall get home, and there I have a tax lawsuit waiting for me, and a complaint about a picture from some noted industrialist, and very soon the firm of Feilchenfeldt & Snakeinthegrass will find out that I have come back without any pictures and give me the boot' (Zurich, 29 July 1929). In August he goes to Scotland with Walter Feilchenfeldt. He spends the winter in Paris.

1930
In January Kokoschka is elected to the Prussian Academy of Arts in Berlin. He spends the spring painting in North Africa and the summer in Italy, mainly in Rome and at Anticoli.

In the autumn the Nazis make their first attacks on 'degenerate art'. The Nazi minister of education in Thuringia, Wilhelm Frick, orders works by Kokoschka to be confiscated from the Schlossmuseum, Weimar. Paul Schultze-Naumburg, in his book *Kunst und Rasse* (Art and Race), compares a portrait by Kokoschka with works by mental patients.

From the end of September onwards Kokoschka is back in Paris.

1931
In January a major retrospective at the Kunsthalle, Mannheim. In February and March Kokoschka exhibits in Paris. Despite favourable reviews, he finds no local market for his paintings.

The world economic crisis affects the art trade. The firm of Cassirer, Kokoschka's gallery for many years past, now seeks to cut back his monthly retainer to a flat 2,000 marks. Coming as it does immediately after the moral and artistic success of the Paris exhibitions, this proposal strikes Kokoschka as demeaning; he refuses and annuls the con-

Fig. 21 Kokoschka at the Villa des Camélias, Paris, 1931

tract. The dispute between him and his gallery is thrashed out in open letters to the *Frankfurter Zeitung* in which he interprets the affair as a difference of principle between art and the art trade. In Kokoschka's view the idea of imposing a minimum output quota on a painter is unconscionable and anti-artistic.

In June, after the suicide of the French painter Jules Pascin, Kokoschka moves into Pascin's house, the Villa des Camélias (see fig. 21). For the first time since the onset of the economic crisis in 1929, he is short of money.

From early September 1931 until March 1932 he is in Vienna (see fig. 22), where he produces a series of paintings and drawings of a Liebhartstal girl, Trudl Bandera (see plates 66, 67). Meier-Graefe (fig. 23) visits him and expresses enthusiasm for his work.

1932

The Galerie Probst in Dresden shows a number of paintings and drawings by Kokoschka, and the resulting sales cushion the worst of his financial distress.

In the summer Kokoschka once more shows at the Venice Biennale, this time in the Austrian pavilion. The first publication of his drawings in book form appears, with a foreword by Paul Westheim (see fig. 24).

1933

Kokoschka stays in Paris until May. He has no income, his health is poor and he is in danger of imprisonment after bouncing a cheque. 'My lung is bad, constant fever, and either in the bronchi or devil knows where else there must be abscesses, because the fever always subsides when I cough blood and pus, whereupon I have a few days' respite. I am undernourished, and of course I have neither a doctor nor any nursing care.... Everyone is just leaving me here to snuff it. Somebody has to come along and get me out of this. I have to be saved from the clutches of the law [over the cheque bouncing] and get something to eat and vanish from this city. The filth here makes my lung more of a mess than ever' (to Ehrenstein, Paris, 18 January 1933).

On 30 January Adolf Hitler becomes Chancellor of the German Reich. The periodical *Deutsche Kulturkorrespondenz* demands the removal from museums of 'all works with a cosmopolitan or Bolshevik tendency'. On 15 February the Prussian Academy of Arts is purged. Many artists go into exile in the U.S.A. or flee to Prague or Paris.

In May the 86-year-old Max Liebermann resigns from the Prussian Academy of Arts in protest at the 'Aryan laws'. Kokoschka publishes an open letter to the *Frankfurter Zeitung*, 'Die Stimme, die Max Liebermann gefehlt hat' (The Voice that Was Never Raised in Defence of Liebermann). In it he unequivocally supports Liebermann's decision. Five paintings by Kokoschka are confiscated from the Dresden state collections, and in Germany he is once and for all anathematized: 'In Italy I get a bet-

Fig. 22   Kokoschka and his brother Bohuslav (left) in the artist's Liebhartstal studio, 1931/2

ter press than Cézanne, and in Germany I get a worse one than Kürten the Cannibal. Humankind is truly so moronic that by the end of one's life one starts to become seriously interested it' (to Ehrenstein, Paris, 18 January 1933).

Kokoschka spends the summer with Consul Bob Gesinus Visser and his wife in Rapallo. Among the works painted there is *Santa Margherita, Harbour* (plate 68). The stay ends with a quarrel: according to Kokoschka, Visser is a rich gigolo 'who bailed me out in Paris and then wanted to turn me into a picture factory, until in the end I had to smack his head for him' (to Ehrenstein, Rapallo, June 1933).

On 23 August Adolf Loos dies. Kokoschka delivers a commemorative address to the Werkbund in Vienna. He moves in with his mother in the Liebhartstal house.

At the end of the year he makes a further public comment on the Nazis' fraudulent cultural mythology; this is a political essay, 'Totem und Tabu: Denkübungen eines Zynikers' (Totem and Taboo: A Cynic's Mental Exercises).

In *Der Wiener Kunstwanderer* Thomas Mann writes of Kokoschka: 'For a long time...I have regarded [him] as the quintessence of modern painting. I love, understand and admire the art of painting in our age first and foremost in his work...civilized magic – that is what it seems to me Kokoschka's pictures embody...he is a skilful dreamer, a master of exact fantasy, in whose magical work the spirit becomes nature and the real grows transparent to the spiritual.'

Fig. 23   Julius Meier-Graefe

Fig. 24   *Paul Westheim*, 1923; lithograph, 31 x 41 cm

PRAGUE, 1934-1938

1934

Lecturing in Budapest on 'The *Via Lucis* of Comenius', Kokoschka calls for citizens to be educated for political maturity. Soon after his return to Vienna civil war breaks out (12-15 February). Workers' housing comes under artillery fire; horrified, Kokoschka wants to leave. Through the Prague art dealer Hugo Feigl he secures permission to paint a portrait of the first president of the Czechoslovak Republic, Tomáš G. Masaryk, then eighty-four years old.

In April the Austrian Chancellor, Engelbert Dollfuss, bans all political parties except the Patriotic Front. In an essay, 'Thomas Paine oder der soziale Staat', Kokoschka registers his protest at the end of Austrian democracy and the advent of authoritarian rule.

On 4 July his mother dies. Deeply upset, Kokoschka seems to have lost some of the will to live: 'Since Mother died, I have taken no real pleasure in living' (to Ehrenstein, late August).

On 25 September he travels to his father's native city, Prague, where his sister Berta has been living since 1918. From Prague he tells Anna Kallin of his artistic unproductivity since leaving Paris: 'In Vienna I almost became a politician at the sight of all those princely gigolos, crusading liberal cannoneers and slap-happy bigots who are setting out to promote the tourist trade . . . by herding the entire rural population of Austria into concentration camps. . . . Instead of stool pigeons, gauleiters and God in the first clause of the constitution, it would be better to introduce Matriarchy and workers' soviets into the elementary schools' (5 October 1934).

Kokoschka decides to settle in Prague (see fig. 25). With his new dealer, Hugo Feigl, he looks for high places from which to paint the city. He paints *Prague, View from the Villa Kramář* (plate 71) and *Prague, View of the Charles Bridge from the Monastery of the Knights of the Cross* (plate 72). One of the houses from which he paints the Charles Bridge is that of Dr K. B. Palkovský; there he meets Olda Palkovská, his future wife (see fig. 26).

1935

In a number of articles and lectures Kokoschka speaks out against the inhumanity of Nazism. In June he paints the portrait of President Masaryk (fig. 27). A law is passed debarring resident aliens from political activity, and Masaryk eases Kokoschka's path to the acquisition of Czechoslovak citizenship. In the autumn Kokoschka founds a 'Union for Justice and Freedom', which opposes the violation of human rights and the destruction of culture, as exemplified by the book-burnings staged by the Nazis. In Germany the book of drawings *Kokoschka: Handzeichnungen*, edited by Ernst Rathenau, is seized on publication.

Fig. 25   Kokoschka on the balcony of his Prague studio, *c.* 1936

Fig. 26   *Olda*, 1935; chalk on paper, 45.5 x 37 cm. Formerly Galerie Würthle, Vienna

1936

In March Kokoschka attends the Brussels Peace Congress as a member of the Czechoslovak delegation. He considers emigrating to the U.S.A.

On 11 July, under a treaty concluded between Hitler and the Austrian chancellor, Kurt von Schuschnigg, Austria is declared to be a 'German State'. In his essay 'Domine quo vadis' Kokoschka warns of the consequences of the Nazi ideology, which 'inevitably leads to the horrors of mass executions, systematic torture and hostage-taking, to the institutionalization of the secret police . . . and to the greatest disgrace of this century, concentration camps'.

Fig. 27
Tomáš G. Masaryk, 1936;
oil on canvas, 97.7 x 131 cm.
Museum of Art,
Carnegie Institute, Pittsburgh

1937

In May and June the Österreichisches Museum für Kunst und Industrie (later Österreichisches Museum für angewandte Kunst) stages the first major Kokoschka retrospective to be held in Vienna. As a protest against 'Austrofascism', Kokoschka refuses to visit the exhibition.

On 19 July the exhibition 'Entartete Kunst' (Degenerate Art) opens in the Hofgarten wing of the Residenz in Munich, where it attracts large crowds until it closes in November. It includes eight works by Kokoschka, one of which is *The Tempest*, from the Kunsthalle, Hamburg. By the end of the year more than four hundred works by Kokoschka have been withdrawn from public collections as 'degenerate art'.

He writes to Chancellor Schuschnigg to demand that the Austrian government take diplomatic measures to protect artistic creation and to resist the pogrom that is being conducted against artists. He also writes the essays 'Entartete Kunst' and 'Der moderne Staat – ein Absurdum'. His poster *Help the Basque Children!* (fig. 1, p. 37), a protest at the horrors of the Spanish Civil War, appears on walls in Bohemia. He paints a portrait of his girlfriend, Olda Palkovská (plate 75), and *Self-Portrait of a Degenerate Artist* (fig. 29).

1938

On 12 March German troops march into Austria. Kokoschka stays in Prague, refusing to leave his sick sister. Many of the collectors who have been buying his work flee into exile, and he once more finds himself in dire financial straits.

In the spring the German Propaganda Ministry puts twenty-four of his paintings up for sale, at home and abroad. On 1 July he is expelled from the Prussian Academy of Arts. In London, from 7 to 31 July, the exhibition 'Modern German Art' is shown as a counter to 'Entartete Kunst'. Kokoschka is represented by twenty-two works.

Kokoschka decides to move to London. He writes to the distinguished champion of modern art, Herbert Read: 'I must start again from scratch, and I therefore need powerful protection and, if possible, a work permit for England. Otherwise I am lost, as your Lords have generously made a present of my own country, Austria, to the Nazis' (Prague, 17 May 1938).

On 29 September Hitler, Chamberlain and Daladier conclude the Munich Agreement, which seals the fate of Czechoslovakia (see *The Red Egg*, plate 80, and *The Crab*, plate 79).

Kokoschka's future wife, Olda Palkovská, presses him to flee from Prague. On 18 October the couple board the last possible flight to London, via Rotterdam. Their trunks are left behind, but there is an unfinished painting in their hand-baggage. In London Kokoschka paints from memory his last Prague picture, *Prague – Nostalgia* (plate 76).

LONDON, 1939-1953

1939

Kokoschka is a founder member of the Free German League of Culture, set up in London on 1 March; other members include John Heartfield, Alfred Kerr and Stefan Zweig. On 13 March the Austrian Centre – Association of Austrians is founded, with Sigmund Freud as its honorary president. In Paris the Galerie Saint-Etienne shows an exhibition of portraits by Kokoschka.

At the Galerie Fischer, Lucerne, on 30 June, there is an auction of paintings by 'degenerate' artists confiscated from German museums. Among the works sold off from the Propaganda Ministry's storehouses is Kokoschka's *The Tempest*, which goes to the Kunstmuseum, Basle.

In early August Kokoschka and Olda move to Polperro in Cornwall (see plate 78).

On 3 September Britain declares war on Germany. Kokoschka paints a series of political allegories in which he reacts to current developments in Europe (see plates 77, 79, 80).

1940-1945

In the summer of 1940 the south coast of England is declared out of bounds to foreigners, and Kokoschka and Olda have to move back to London. Being Czechoslovak citizens, however, they are treated (unlike the German and Austrian émigrés) as friendly rather than enemy aliens. From autumn 1940 onwards Kokoschka and Edith Hoffmann discuss plans for a comprehensive biography of the artist.

On 15 May 1941 Olda Palkovská and Oskar Kokoschka are married in an air-raid shelter in London.

In the summer of 1941 Kokoschka becomes president of the Free German League of Culture. In September and October he and Olda are in Scotland. He joins the Free Austrian Movement, which campaigns for the restoration of a free and independent Austria, and gives particular support to its youth group, Young Austria. He calls for the release of those Austrians still interned in British camps.

Between 1940 and 1942 a number of Kokoschka exhibitions are held in the U.S.A., including one-man shows in Saint Louis and Chicago. The portrait of President Masaryk is sold in the U.S.A., and he puts $ 4,000 of the proceeds into the newly founded Oskar Kokoschka Fund of War Orphans of all Nations United in Liberated Czechoslovakia (see fig. 28). On 25 October 1942 Kokoschka makes a controversial, pro-Soviet speech to the Free German League of Culture to commemorate the twenty-fifth anniversary of the founding of the Soviet Union. During the war he makes a number of pronouncements on educational matters, and in particular on that of the re-education of young Nazis in Germany after the war.

Fig. 28 *Christ Helps the Starving Children*, 1945/6; poster

Fig. 29
Self-Portrait of a Degenerate Artist, 1937; oil on canvas, 110 x 76 cm. Private collection (on loan to the Scottish National Gallery of Modern Art, Edinburgh)

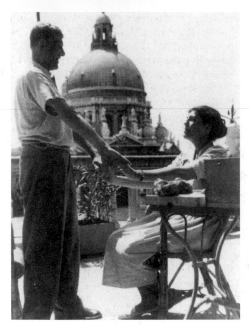

Fig. 30   The Kokoschkas, Venice, summer 1948

Back in Scotland in the spring of 1944, he produces a large number of crayon sketches.

The Kunstmuseum, Berne, holds a *Der Sturm* exhibition, which includes twenty-two works by Kokoschka.

On 7 May 1945 Germany surrenders unconditionally. In response to the devastation of Europe Kokoschka writes the essay 'Das Wesen der Österreichischen Kunst' (The Essence of Austrian Art). Once more, the Kokoschkas spend the summer and autumn in Scotland.

From 15 September to 1 November 1945 the Neue Galerie in Vienna shows drawings and prints by Klimt, Schiele and Kokoschka – who repeatedly tells his biographer, Edith Hoffmann, to leave Austrian art, Klimt excluded, out of her book altogether: 'But nothing by Viennese daubers, except for Klimt!' (North Wales, 15 April 1943). He lays great stress on his own total originality and the impossibility of making comparisons: 'If it had been the way you describe it, I would at the very least have had to hang around museums and libraries and academies all my life.... All very well for the likes of your precious Schiele, of course, but in my case well below my cost price. There are myriads of mayflies, but my life is unique' (to Edith Hoffmann, London, November 1943).

1946-1953

On his sixtieth birthday, 1 March 1946, Kokoschka receives numerous tributes from Vienna, including a ten-page telegram from the city's mayor, Theodor Körner, asking him to reorganize the Kunstgewerbeschule and the Austrian educational system.

In February 1947 Kokoschka assumes British nationality. A major retrospective exhibition of his works is held in March at the Kunstmuseum, Basle, and in July at the Kunsthaus, Zurich. In London there appears the first monograph on his work to contain a – provisional – *catalogue raisonné*: *Oskar Kokoschka: Life and Work* by Edith Hoffmann.

In September 1947 Kokoschka is on the Riffelalp, near Zermatt, where he paints *Matterhorn I* (plate 81). In October he visits his brother Bohuslav in Vienna and attempts – with the support of Mayor Körner and of a city councillor, Victor Matejka – to regain possession of his house in Liebhartstal, requisitioned under the Nazis. An interview, syndicated under the title 'Vater der modernen Kunst?' (Father of Modern Art?), attracts considerable attention.

In the summer of 1948 the Kokoschkas are in Venice for the Biennale (see fig. 30), 'where I, together with Van Gogh, am to show a life's work' (to Victor Matejka, London, 15 January 1948). The Kokoschka show is an international success. He paints *Venice, Punta della Dogana with View of San Giorgio* (plate 82). From September to December the Kokoschkas are in Florence; he paints *Self-Portrait (Fiesole)* (plate 83).

In the U.S.A., in 1948, there is a major touring retrospective (Boston, Washington, Saint Louis, San Francisco, Wilmington and New York). In September and October the Haus der Kunst in Munich presents another retrospective, the first exhibition of Kokoschka's work in Germany since the war.

On 4 November 1951 the Kokoschkas buy a plot of land at Villeneuve on Lake Geneva. Kokoschka's birthplace, Pöchlarn, awards him honorary citizenship.

In 1952 he is represented for the fourth time at the Venice Biennale.

Fig. 31   Kokoschka teaching his course The School of Seeing at the International Summer Academy of Visual Art, Salzburg, *c.* 1956

VILLENEUVE, 1953-1980

1953

On the initiative of Kokoschka and of the gallery owner Friedrich Welz an international summer art academy (Internationale Sommerakademie für Bildende Künste) is inaugurated in Salzburg on 10 July 1953. Every summer until 1963 Kokoschka conducts the course that he calls The School of Seeing (see fig. 31): 'In Salzburg I collect together... pupils from all over the world, in order to arouse in their minds and hearts the ability to see with their own eyes, an ability that standardized modern education is visibly causing most people to lose.'

On 9 September the Kokoschkas move into their new house, Villa Delphin, at Villeneuve (see fig. 33, 34).

1955-1962

Kokoschka designs sets and costumes for a production of Mozart's *The Magic Flute* at the 1955 Salzburg Festival.

In the spring of 1956 he travels to Greece, where – as on later Mediterranean trips – he

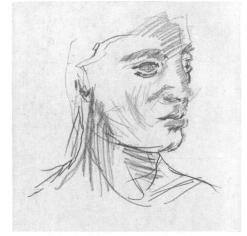

Fig. 32   *Head of a Goddess from a Metope of the Hera Temple at Selinunte*, 1959; pencil on paper, 35.3 x 25.3 cm. Private collection

draws metopes, funerary stelae and other sculptures (see fig. 32). In June he paints *Vienna, State Opera* (fig. 10, p. 34) for the Austrian Ministry of Education.

Hans Maria Wingler edits Kokoschka's writings of 1907 to 1955 and compiles the first fully documented *catalogue raisonné*.

In March 1958 there is a major retrospective at the Haus der Kunst in Munich, including 153 paintings and a total of 276 prints and drawings. From May to July the Künstlerhaus in Vienna stages the largest Kokoschka exhibition ever, with a catalogue containing 682 items. In 1960 an exhibition of late work, 'Der späte Kokoschka', is shown in Brunswick and Bremen, and in London the Marlborough Gallery has 'Kokoschka in England and Scotland'. In 1962, also in London, there is a large retrospective at the Tate Gallery.

From 1960 to 1962 Kokoschka designs sets and costumes for three plays by Ferdinand Raimund, *Moissasurs Zauberfluch, Die gefesselte Phantasie* and *Die unheilbringende Krone*, at the Burgtheater in Vienna.

1963 - 1969

In Florence, in the spring of 1963, Kokoschka designs sets and costumes for a production of Verdi's *Un ballo in maschera* at the Maggio Musicale Fiorentino. In Oxford he is awarded an honorary doctorate.

In 1965 he designs sets and costumes for a production of *The Magic Flute* at the Grand Théâtre, Geneva; they are based on drawings originally intended for a staging at the Royal Opera House, Covent Garden, in London.

On the occasion of his eightieth birthday, in 1966, he receives many honours: the Marlborough Gallery in London shows 'Homage to Oskar Kokoschka', and the Staatsgalerie in Stuttgart has an exhibition of watercolours and drawings. In the summer there is a large retrospective at the Kunsthaus in Zurich. In June Kokoschka paints a view of the still

largely devastated city centre of Berlin for the publisher Axel Springer.

In 1967 he produces a cycle of etchings, *Die Frösche* (*The Frogs*), as a protest against the advent of a military dictatorship in Greece. The allusion to Aristophanes' play is taken up the following year in a painting, *The Frogs* (plate 93), which is Kokoschka's indictment of the Soviet invasion of Czechoslovakia.

1970 - 1980

At Villeneuve, in February 1970, Kokoschka starts work on his autobiography, *Mein Leben* (*My Life*). He is elected an honorary member of the Royal Academy of Arts, London.

His eighty-fifth birthday, in 1971, is marked by a retrospective at the Oberes Belvedere in Vienna. That winter, at Villeneuve, he embarks on his last self-portrait, *Time, Gentlemen, Please* (plate 95). In June 1973 the Oskar Kokoschka-Dokumentation, Pöchlarn, is opened in the house where he was born.

In the summer of 1974 he develops an eye complaint, for which he undergoes an operation the following year. He now devotes most of his time to revising and correcting his writings, which are being prepared for publication. In 1975 Hans Maria Wingler and Friedrich Welz publish a catalogue of his prints, *Oskar Kokoschka: Das druckgraphische Werk*.

In 1975 the Austrian Chancellor, Bruno Kreisky, persuades Kokoschka to resume Austrian citizenship.

Kokoschka's ninetieth birthday is celebrated in 1976 with exhibitions in Salzburg (Galerie Welz), Munich (Bayerische Akademie der Schönen Künste) and Athens, and by an honorary doctorate from the Philosophy Faculty of Salzburg University. In 1978 a major exhibition of 450 works is held in Japan, at Kamakura (near Tokyo) and at Kyoto.

Oskar Kokoschka dies in hospital in Montreux on 22 February 1980. He is buried at Clarens, near Villeneuve, on 27 February.

Fig. 33   Villa Delphin at Villeneuve, the Kokoschkas' home from 1953 onwards

Fig. 34   The Kokoschkas at Villeneuve, *c.* 1975

Fig. 35
Self-Portrait with Olda, 1963;
oil on canvas, 89 x 115.5 cm.
Salzburger Landessammlungen – Rupertinum, Salzburg

Selected Bibliography

Plays and other Writings by the Artist

Dramen und Bilder, intro. Paul Stefan, Leipzig, Kurt Wolff, 1913. Includes the plays *Mörder Hoffnung der Frauen, Sphinx und Strohmann* and *Schauspiel.*

Der brennende Dornbusch, Mörder Hoffnung der Frauen, Leipzig, Kurt Wolff, 1917. Also contains *Der Jüngste Tag* and *41.*

Vier Dramen, Berlin, Paul Cassirer, 1919. Contains the plays *Orpheus und Eurydike, Der brennende Dornbusch, Mörder Hoffnung der Frauen* and *Hiob.*

'Der Fetisch', in *Künstlerbekenntnisse*, ed. Paul Westheim, pp. 243 - 54, Berlin, Ullstein, 1925. Contains nine letters of 1918/19 to Hermine Moos about the making of the doll.

Schriften 1907-1955, ed. Hans M. Wingler, Munich, Langen-Müller, 1956.

Spur im Treibsand: Geschichten (1956), trans. as *A Sea Ringed with Visions*, London, Thames and Hudson, 1962.

Mein Leben (1971), trans. as *My Life*, London, Thames and Hudson, 1974.

Das schriftliche Werk, ed. Heinz Spielmann, vol. 1, *Dichtungen und Dramen*, vol. 2, *Erzählungen*, vol. 3, *Aufsätze, Vorträge, Essays zur Kunst*, vol. 4, *Politische Äusserungen*, Hamburg, Christians, 1973 - 6.

Oskar Kokoschka: Vom Erlebnis im Leben, ed. Otto Breicha, Salzburg, Verlag Galerie Welz, 1976.

Briefe, ed. Olda Kokoschka and Heinz Spielmann, vol. 1, *1905-1919*, vol. 2, *1919-1934*, vol. 3, *1934-1953*, vol. 4, *1953-1976*, Düsseldorf, Claassen, 1984, 1985, 1986, 1988.

Portfolios and Illustrated Books by the Artist

Jagdbuch (Diarium), Vienna, Wiener Werkstätte, 1908.

Die träumenden Knaben, Vienna, Verlag der Wiener Werkstätte, 1908. With eight colour lithographs (Wingler/Welz 22 - 29).

Ehrenstein, Albert, *Tubutsch*, Vienna, Jahoda & Siegel, 1911. With twelve line etchings after drawings by the artist.

Zwanzig Zeichnungen, Berlin, Verlag Der Sturm, 1913.

Die chinesische Mauer, Leipzig, Kurt Wolff, 1914. Published in book form and as a portfolio of eight lithographs of 1913 (Wingler/Welz 35 - 42) illustrating Karl Kraus's essay.

Der gefesselte Kolumbus, Berlin, Fritz Gurlitt. Two portfolio editions, 1916 and 1918, each with twelve lithographs (Wingler/Welz 43 - 54) illustrating Kokoschka's dramatic poem. Published in book form in the series *Die Neuen Bilderbücher* (3rd series), Berlin, Fritz Gurlitt, 1921.

Menschenköpfe, Berlin, Verlag Der Sturm, 1916.

Mörder Hoffnung der Frauen, Berlin, Verlag Der Sturm, 1916.

O Ewigkeit – Du Donnerwort (Bach Cantata), Berlin, Fritz Gurlitt. Two portfolio editions, 1916/17 and 1918, and one bound edition, 1918, with eleven lithographs of 1914 (Wingler/Welz 58 - 68) illustrating the words of J. S. Bach's Cantata No. 60, 'O Ewigkeit – Du Donnerwort'.

Hiob, Berlin, Paul Cassirer, 1917. Fourteen lithographs of 1916 and 1917 (Wingler/Welz 87 - 100) illustrating Kokoschka's play.

Variationen über ein Thema, ed. Bohuslav Kokoschka, with a foreword by Max Dvořák, Vienna, Lanyi, and Vienna, Prague and Leipzig, Strache, 1921. Portfolio with ten collotype reproductions of drawings by Kokoschka of Camilla Svoboda.

Ann Eliza Reed, Hamburg, Maximilian-Presse, 1952. Story with eleven lithographs (Wingler/Welz 188 - 98).

Shakespeare, King Lear, London, Ganymed Original Editions, 1963. Boxed edition with sixteen lithographs (Wingler/Welz 223 - 38). Published in book form, with the lithographs reproduced in reduced size, by Verlag C. J. Bucher, Lucerne and Frankfurt am Main, 1971.

Bekenntnis zu Hellas, London, Marlborough Fine Art, 1964. Twenty-six lithographs (Wingler/Welz 242 - 67) in two boxes.

Apulia, London, Marlborough Fine Art, 1964. Boxed edition of twenty lithographs (Wingler/Welz 268 - 87).

Die Odyssee, London, Ganymed Original Editions and Marlborough Fine Art, 1965. Boxed edition of forty-four lithographs (Wingler/Welz 294 - 338).

Marrakesch, London, Marlborough Fine Art, 1966. Boxed edition of eighteen lithographs (Wingler/Welz 339 - 56).

Saul and David, London, Ganymed Original Editions and Marlborough Fine Art, 1969. Boxed edition of forty-one lithographs (Wingler/Welz 392 - 432). Published in book form, with the lithographs reproduced in reduced size, by Verlag C. J. Bucher, Lucerne and Frankfurt am Main, 1970, and, in an English edition, by Thames and Hudson, London, 1973.

'Die Frösche' des Aristophanes, Frankfurt am Main, Verlag Ars librorum – Gotthard de Beauclair, 1969. Boxed and bound editions with twelve drypoints (Wingler/Welz 437 - 48).

Penthesilea, Frankfurt am Main, Verlag Ars librorum – Gotthard Beauclair, 1970. Boxed edition of ten drypoints (Wingler/Welz 454 - 63) illustrating Heinrich von Kleist's play.

Pan, Hamburg, Hoffmann & Campe, 1978. Boxed edition of seventeen lithographs (Wingler/Welz 543 - 49, 560) illustrating Knut Hamsun's novel.

Books and Articles

Axel Springer Verlag (ed.), *Oskar Kokoschka malt Berlin*, Berlin, 1966.

Biermann, Georg, *Oskar Kokoschka*, Junge Kunst, vol. 52, Leipzig and Berlin, 1929.

Bisanz, Hans, 'Oskar Kokoschka: Vom "heiligen" zum wilden Frühling', in *Traum und Wirklichkeit*, exhibition catalogue, Vienna, Künstlerhaus Wien, 1985.

Borchert, Bernhard, *Kokoschka*, London, 1960.

Borowitz, Helen, 'Youth as Metaphor and Image in Wedekind, Kokoschka and Schiele', *Art Journal*, vol. 33, no. 3 (Spring 1974), pp. 219 - 25.

Brandt, Regina, 'Figurationen und Kompositionen in den Dramen Oskar Kokoschkas', Ph. D. thesis, Munich, 1965.

Bultmann, Bernhard, *Oskar Kokoschka*, London, 1961.

Denkler, Horst, 'Die Druckfassungen der Dramen Oskar Kokoschkas', *Deutsche Vierteljahrsschrift für Literaturwissenschaft und Geistesgeschichte*, vol. 40, no. 1 (1966), pp. 90 - 108.

Fenjö, Ivan, *Oskar Kokoschka: Die frühe Graphik*, Vienna, 1976.

Gatt, Giuseppe, *Kokoschka*, London, New York, Sydney and Toronto, 1971.

Goldscheider, Ludwig, in collaboration with the artist, *Kokoschka*, London, 1963.

Gombrich, Ernst H., *Kokoschka in his Time*, Tate Modern Masters, London, 1986.

Gordon, Donald E., 'Oskar Kokoschka and the Visionary Tradition', in Gerald Chapple and Hans H. Schulte (eds), *The Turn of the Century: German Literature and Art, 1890-1915*, pp. 23 - 52, Bonn, 1981.

Gorsen, Peter, 'Kokoschka und die Puppe', in *Oskar Kokoschka: Symposion*, pp. 187 - 202, Salzburg and Vienna, 1986.

Heilmaier, Hans, *Kokoschka*, Les Artistes Nouveaux, Paris, 1929.

Hevesi, Ludwig, *Altkunst – Neukunst: Wien 1894-1908*, Vienna, 1909.

Hodin, Joseph P. (ed.), *Bekenntnis zu Kokoschka: Erinnerungen und Deutungen*, Berlin and Mainz, 1963.

Hodin, Joseph P., *Kokoschka und Hellas*, Vienna, 1975.

Hodin, Joseph P., *Oskar Kokoschka: The Artist and his Time*, London, 1966; trans. and rev. as *Oskar Kokoschka: Sein Leben, seine Zeit*, Mainz and Berlin, 1968.

Hodin, Joseph P., *Oskar Kokoschka: Eine Psychographie*, Vienna, etc., 1971.

Hodin, Joseph P., 'Style and Personality: A Graphological Portrait of Oskar Kokoschka', *Art Quarterly*, vol. 8 (1945), pp. 303 - 16.

Hoffmann, Edith, *Kokoschka: Life and Work*, London, 1947. With two essays by the artist and a foreword by Herbert Read.

Hofmann, Werner, 'Der irrende Ritter', in *Oskar Kokoschka: Symposion*, pp. 265 - 78, Salzburg and Vienna, 1986.

Hofmann, Werner, 'Oskar Kokoschka', *Wort in der Zeit*, vol. 2, no. 3 (1956), pp. 1 - 11.

Horstmann, Edgar, *Oskar Kokoschka in Hamburg*, Hamburg, 1965.

Kamm, Otto, 'Oskar Kokoschka und das Theater', Ph. D. thesis, Vienna, 1958.

Kasten, Walter, 'Wie Oskar Kokoschka die "Linzer Landschaft" malte', *Linz aktiv*, no. 76 (1980), pp. 55 - 64.

Krapf-Weiler, Almut, 'Zur Bedeutung des österreichischen Barock für Oskar Kokoschka', *Wiener Jahrbuch für Kunstgeschichte*, vol. 40 (1987), pp. 195 - 208.

Leshko, Jaroslaw, 'Oskar Kokoschka: Paintings 1907-1915', Ph. D. thesis, New York, Columbia University, 1977. University Microfilms International, Ann Arbor, Michigan, and London, 1982.

Lischka, Gerhard J., *Oskar Kokoschka, Maler und Dichter: Eine literar-ästhetische Untersuchung zu seiner Doppelbegabung*, Europäische Hochschulschriften, Reihe Vergleichende Literaturwissenschaften, vol. 4, Berne and Frankfurt am Main, 1972.

Mahler-Werfel, Alma, *Mein Leben*, Frankfurt am Main, 1960.

Masciotta, Michelangelo, *Disegni di Kokoschka*, Florence, 1942.

Masciotta, Michelangelo, *Kokoschka*, Maestri Moderni, Florence, 1949.

Myers, Bernard S., *Malerei des Expressionismus: Eine Generation im Aufbruch*, Cologne, 1957.

Netzer, Remigius, *Oskar Kokoschka: Lithographien*, Munich, 1956.

Oskar Kokoschka: Symposion, ed. Erika Patka, Salzburg and Vienna, 1986. Symposium held at the Hochschule für angewandte Kunst, Vienna, from 3 to 7 March 1986 to mark the centenary of the artist's birth.

Oskar Kokoschka: Thermopylae, intro. Carl G. Heise, with texts by the artist and Bruno Snell, Werkmonographien zur bildenden Kunst in Reclams Universal-Bibliothek, vol. 68, Stuttgart, 1961.

Oskar Kokoschka: Thermopylae – Ein Triptychon, with texts by the artist and Walter Kern, Winterthur, 1955.

Oskar Kokoschka: Watercolours, Drawings, Writings, intro. John Russell, London, 1962.

Platschek, Hans, *Oskar Kokoschka*, Biblioteca Argentina de Arte, Buenos Aires, 1946.

Radford, Robert, 'Kokoschka's Political Allegories', *Art Monthly* (June 1986), pp. 3 - 6.

Rathenau, Ernst (ed.), *Kokoschka: Handzeichnungen*, Berlin, 1935. The original foreword, by Paul Westheim, was replaced by the artist's 'Lebensgeschichte' in most copies.

Rathenau, Ernst (ed.), in collaboration with the artist, *Oskar Kokoschka: Handzeichnungen 1906-1965*, with a foreword by Carl G. Heise, New York and Hamburg, 1966.

Rathenau, Ernst (ed.), in collaboration with the artist, *Oskar Kokoschka: Handzeichnungen 1906-1969*, with a foreword by Carl G. Heise, New York and Hamburg, 1971.

Rathenau, Ernst (ed.), *Oskar Kokoschka: Handzeichnungen*, vol. 5, New York and Hamburg, 1977.

Rathenau, Ernst, *Der Zeichner Kokoschka*, with a foreword by Paul Westheim, New York, 1961.

Reisinger, Alfred, *Kokoschkas Dichtungen nach dem Expressionismus*, Beiträge zur österreichischen Kultur- und Geistesgeschichte, vol. 2, Vienna, Munich and Zurich, 1978.

Sabarsky, Serge, *Oskar Kokoschka: Early Drawings and Watercolours*, London, 1985.

Schmalenbach, Fritz, *Oskar Kokoschka*, Die blauen Bücher, Königstein im Taunus, 1967.

Schmied, Wieland, 'Der Fetisch: Oskar Kokoschkas Selbstbildnis mit Puppe', in idem, *Nach Klimt: Schriften zur Kunst in Österreich*, pp. 53 - 57, Salzburg, 1979.

Schorske, Carl E., 'Explosion in the Garden: Kokoschka and Schoenberg', in idem, *Fin-de-siècle Vienna: Politics and Culture*, pp. 322 - 66, New York, 1980.

Schvey, Henry I., *Oskar Kokoschka: The Painter as Playwright*, Detroit, 1982.

Schweiger, Werner J., *Der junge Kokoschka: Leben und Werk 1904-1914*, Schriftenreihe der Oskar Kokoschka-Dokumentation Pöchlarn, vol. 1, Vienna and Munich, 1983.

Secci, Lia, 'Die lyrischen Dichtungen Oskar Kokoschkas', *Jahrbuch der deutschen Schillergesellschaft*, vol. 12 (1968), pp. 457-92.

Spielmann, Heinz, 'Kokoschkas Bilder der europäischen Städte', *Europäische Hefte*, no. 1 (1974), pp. 69-72.

Spielmann, Heinz, *Oskar Kokoschka: Die Fächer für Alma Mahler*, Hamburg, 1969, repr. as *Kokoschkas Fächer für Alma Mahler*, Die bibliophilen Taschenbücher, vol. 462, Dortmund, 1985.

Stegen, Ina, *Das schönste Atelier der Welt: 25 Jahre Internationale Sommerakademie für Bildende Kunst, Salzburg*, Salzburg, 1978.

Thurston, Doris, *Notes on Kokoschka*, New York, 1950.

Tietze, Hans, 'Der Fall Kokoschka', *Der Kreis*, vol. 7, no. 2 (1930), pp. 81-85.

Tietze, Hans, 'Oskar Kokoschka', *Zeitschrift für bildende Kunst*, n. s., vol. 29, nos. 4/5 (January/February 1918), pp. 83-97.

Tietze, Hans, 'Oskar Kokoschkas neue Werke', *Die bildenden Künste*, vol. 2, nos. 11/12 (1919), pp. 249-56.

Tomeš, Jan, *Oskar Kokoschka: The Artist in Prague*, London, 1967.

Tomeš, Jan, *Oskar Kokoschka: London Views, British Landscapes*, London, 1972.

Vergo, Peter, *Art in Vienna 1898-1918: Klimt, Kokoschka, Schiele and their Contemporaries*, London, 1975.

Wacha, Georg, *Oskar Kokoschka in Linz: Eine Dokumentation*, Linz, 1986.

Welz, Friedrich, *Oskar Kokoschka: Frühe Druckgraphik, 1906-1912*, Salzburg, 1977.

Westheim, Paul *Oskar Kokoschka: Gestalten und Landschaften*, Zurich, 1952.

Westheim, Paul, *Oskar Kokoschka: Landschaften*, Zurich, 1948.

Westheim, Paul, *Oskar Kokoschka: Landschaften*, vol. 2, Zurich, 1959.

Westheim, Paul, *Oskar Kokoschka: Das Werk Kokoschkas in 62 Abbildungen*, Potsdam and Berlin, 1918.

Westheim, Paul, *Oskar Kokoschka: Das Werk Kokoschkas in 135 Abbildungen*, Berlin, 1925.

Whitford, Frank, *Oskar Kokoschka: A Life*, London, 1986.

Wild, Doris, *Moderne Malerei: Ihre Entwicklung seit dem Impressionismus, 1880-1950*, Zurich, 1950.

Wild, Doris, *Oskar Kokoschka: Blumenaquarelle*, Zurich, 1948.

Wingler, Hans Maria, *Introduction to Kokoschka*, London, 1958.

Wingler, Hans Maria, *Künstler und Poeten: Zeichnungen von Oskar Kokoschka*, Feldafing, 1954.

Wingler, Hans Maria (ed.), *Oskar Kokoschka: Ein Lebensbild*, Ullstein-Buch, no. 549, Berlin, 1966.

Wingler, Hans Maria (ed.), *Oskar Kokoschka: Ein Lebensbild in zeitgenössischen Dokumenten*, Munich, 1956.

Wingler, Hans Maria, *Oskar Kokoschka: Orbis pictus I und II*, Salzburg, 1951.

Wingler, Hans Maria, *Oskar Kokoschka: The Work of the Painter*, London, 1958.

Wingler, Hans Maria, and Friedrich Welz, *Oskar Kokoschka: Das druckgraphische Werk*, 2 vols, Salzburg, 1975, 1981.

Exhibition Catalogues (after 1945)

Barcelona, Museu Picasso, *Oskar Kokoschka 1886-1980*, 1988.

Basle, Kunsthalle, *Oskar Kokoschka*, intro. Fritz Schmalenbach, 1947.

Berlin, Kupferstichkabinett und Sammlung der Zeichnungen der Staatlichen Museen zu Berlin and Kulturbund der DDR, Stiftung Olda Kokoschka, *Oskar Kokoschka: Graphik und Zeichnungen*, 1983.

Bordeaux, Galerie des Beaux-Arts, *Oskar Kokoschka 1886-1980*, by Gilberte Martin-Mery, with contributions by Werner Hofmann et al., 1983.

Boston, Institute of Contemporary Art, *Oskar Kokoschka*, intro. James Plaut, 1948.

Bregenz, Künstlerhaus Palais Thurn und Taxis, *Oskar Kokoschka*, 1976.

Brunswick, Haus Salve Hospes, *Der späte Kokoschka*, 1960.

Florence, Centro Mostre di Firenze, *Oskar Kokoschka: Dipinti e disegni*, selected by Serge Sabarsky, 1987.

Ghent, Museum voor Schone Kunste, *Oskar Kokoschka*, comp. Serge Sabarsky, with contributions by Otto Breicha, Hilde Haider-Pregler, Mario Praz, Armin A. Wallas et al., 1987.

Hamburg, B. A. T.-Haus und Kunsthaus, *Oskar Kokoschka: Gemälde und Aquarelle seit 1953*, by Heinz Spielmann, 1975.

Kamakurka, Museum of Modern Art, *Oskar Kokoschka*, intro. Heinz Spielmann, 1978.

Karlsruhe, Badischer Kunstverein, *Oskar Kokoschka: Das Porträt*, intro. Klaus Gallwitz, 1966.

London, Marlborough Fine Art, *Oskar Kokoschka (1886-1980): The Late Work*, with contributions by Ernst H. Gombrich, Heinz Spielmann and Katharina Schulz, 1990.

London, Marlborough Gallery, *Oskar Kokoschka: Cityscapes and Landscapes – A 90th Birthday Tribute*, 1976.

London, Tate Gallery, *Kokoschka*, with contributions by Ernst H. Gombrich, Joseph P. Hodin, Fritz Novotny, Hans M. Wingler et al., 1962.

London, Tate Gallery, *Oskar Kokoschka 1886-1980*, cat. by Richard Calvocoressi, with contributions by Werner Hofmann, Peter Vergo and Yvonne Modlin, Heinz Spielmann, Georg Eisler, Alfred Marnau and Katharina Schulz, 1986.

Munich, Haus der Kunst, *Oskar Kokoschka: Aus seinem Schaffen 1907-1950*, 1950.

Munich, Haus der Kunst, *Oskar Kokoschka*, 1958.

New York, Marlborough-Gerson Gallery, *Oskar Kokoschka*, intro. Ernst H. Gombrich, 1966.

Pöchlarn, Oskar Kokoschka-Dokumentation im Geburtshaus des Künstlers, *Oskar Kokoschka: Gemälde und Graphik 1908-1976*, 1980.

Pöchlarn, Oskar Kokoschka-Dokumentation im Geburtshaus des Künstlers, *Oskar Kokoschka: Reiseskizzen aus Schottland und Wales 1942-1945*, 1982.

Pöchlarn, Oskar Kokoschka-Dokumentation im Geburtshaus des Künstlers, *Oskar Kokoschka: 'Der Sturm' – Die Berliner Jahre 1910-1916*, by Werner J. Schweiger, 1986.

Rome, Palazzo Venezia, *Oskar Kokoschka 1886-1980*, with contributions by Carmine Benincasa and Walter Zettl, 1981/82.

Salzburg, Residenzgalerie, *Oskar Kokoschka: Bilder zum Leben*, 1980/81.

Salzburg, Salzburger Landessammlungen, Moderne Galerie, Graphische Sammlung Rupertinum, *Oskar Kokoschka: Das druckgraphische Werk 1906-1975*, 1976.

Vevey, Musée Jenisch, *Hommage à Oskar Kokoschka 1886-1980*, 1984.

Vienna, Historisches Museum der Stadt Wien, *Oskar Kokoschka: Die frühen Jahre – Zeichnungen und Aquarelle*, selected by Serge Sabarsky, 1982/83.

Vienna, Kunstforum, *Oskar Kokoschka*, ed. Klaus Albrecht Schröder and Johann Winkler, with essays by Christoph Asendorf, Ingried Brugger, Edwin Lachnit and Johann Winkler, 1991.

Vienna, Künstlerhaus, *Oskar Kokoschka*, 1958.

Vienna, Museum des 20. Jahrhunderts, *Oskar Kokoschka 1886-1980*, 1982.

Vienna, Österreichische Galerie im Oberen Belvedere, *Oskar Kokoschka zum 85. Geburtstag*, intro. Fritz Novotny, 1971.

Vienna, Österreichisches Museum für angewandte Kunst, *Oskar Kokoschka: Selbstportraits*, organized by the Hochschule für angewandte Kunst, Vienna, and the Oskar Kokoschka-Dokumentation, Pöchlarn, with contributions by Oswald Oberhuber, Heinz Spielmann, Gabriele Koller et al., 1986.

Vienna, Wiener Secession, *Kokoschka*, with an essay by Werner Hofmann, 1955.

Zurich, Kunsthaus, *Oskar Kokoschka*, with an essay by Carl G. Heise, 1966.

List of Plates